"Your next personal ministry diagnosis with 'Drs.' Craig and Carolyn will be completely thorough, mostly painless, and powerfully revealing. Their prognosis of your "staff infection" is to be taken seriously, and the recommended prescriptions could save your life and ministry. Don't miss this appointment."

—Dr. Doug Fagerstrom, president, Grand Rapids
Theological Seminary

"With honesty and humor and a willingness to be vulnerable about their own failures and struggles, Craig and Carolyn have provided an accessible book that provides practical help to those involved in any kind of organization. Their use of a medical model provides a creative way of tackling this area and invites us to observe the 'staff infections' that are present in many communities."

—Dr. Rod Wilson, president, Regent College

"The most practical book ever written for staff leadership—church, organization, and even business. The Willifords' *How to Treat a Staff Infection* is invaluable for all of us that give direction to staff teams. We all face the challenges described in this book. They give clear direction in addressing these situations in productive ways."

—Dave Travis, executive vice president, Leadership Network

"The Willifords offer great antibiotics to administer if you run into complicated situations with your staff, or better yet, preventive and preemptive methods for avoiding problems that can destroy a ministry. I highly recommend this book for those who manage a church staff or think they might in the future. *How to Treat a Staff Infection* gives us the opportunity to create a working environment where the only infectious symptoms spreading are the grace and love of Christ."

—Randy Frazee, teaching pastor, Willow Creek Community
Church; author of *The Connecting Church*

"Craig and I served together on our church staff for seven years, and I greatly admire his diagnostic skills. I just did not realize he was taking medical notes! Those notes and diagnoses of seventeen staff diseases are as real and clear as can be, and the recognizable symptoms will be helpful in any size or style of ministry. All staff leaders should study the careful remedies and practical steps here. The germs are everywhere."

—Knute Larson, senior pastor, The Chapel

D1081663

How to Treat a
Staff Infection

Resolving Problems in Your Church or Ministry Team

Dr. Craig Williford and
Carolyn Williford

BakerBooks

Grand Rapids, Michigan

Published by Baker Books
a division of Baker Publishing Group
P.O. Box 6287, Grand Rapids, MI 49516-6287
www.bakerbooks.com

Printed in the United States of America

Library of Congress Cataloging-in-Publication Data
Williford, Craig.
    How to treat a staff infection : resolving problems in your church or ministry team / Craig Williford and Carolyn Williford.
        p.   cm.
    ISBN 10: 0-8010-6757-X (pbk.)
    ISBN 978-0-8010-6757-0 (pbk.)
    1. Church personnel management. I. Williford, Carolyn. II. Title.
BV652.13.W55 2007
254—dc22   2006032971

I am deeply indebted and thankful
to all the paid and unpaid staff
whom I've had the privilege of serving with over the
past thirty-three years of vocational ministry.
It has been an enjoyable and wild ride.
If you are one of these people,
please add your name
to the line below.
This book is dedicated to you:

_____

Contents

Introduction

How to Treat a Staff Infection

The following are both true statements:

Serving with staff has been one of the most remarkable, rewarding, and enjoyable aspects of my thirty years of vocational ministry.

Serving with staff has been one of the most challenging, draining, and frustrating aspects of my thirty years of vocational ministry.

Think those two sentences are completely contradictory? Well, of course they are—not! Seriously, those who have served on a staff or have supervised staff know that many times these sentences are concurrently true.

For clarity, for the purpose of this book, I am defining *staff* to include both paid and unpaid people who serve in a ministry—whether a church or a parachurch organization. My personal experiences of serving with staff have been quite varied: one experience was totally volunteer; another included two paid and a couple dozen unpaid staff; yet another involved over two hundred paid staff and thousands of unpaid staff. Additionally, I have served as the supervisor of a portion of a staff and of an entire staff. I have also served as a general member of a staff with limited supervisory duties. And finally, my past experience includes both church and academic settings. (There's a future book idea—the similarities and differences between academic staff and church staff.)

The following chapters describe fictional stories and characters loosely adapted from my real-life experiences or the experiences of my friends. The names and details have been changed considerably to ensure confidentiality. Following these case studies, I attempt to provide wise principles that will be transferable to similar situations—hopefully, *your* specific situations. You may find it helpful to use these case studies with a group of people, brainstorming how you might lead through these staff challenges. The organization of this book follows a medical approach of formulating a careful diagnosis and then designing treatment to fit that specific illness. When using the included stories as case studies, you may wish to start the group discussion with diagnosis and then move to treatment.

However, I offer the following important caution before you read the rest of the book and seek to apply these case studies and principles: *Please remember that while many similarities may exist, no two situations are exactly alike.* You must prayerfully seek God for insight into how any of the suggested principles may apply to your particular staff challenges. Hopefully, many will apply. However, I have not offered formulas that work in every case—or that should be followed like a recipe to ensure certain outcomes. Instead, I attempt to provide proven, wise principles that must be carefully adapted to meet your situation.

Godly wisdom can't be reduced to formulaic, robotic applications so that we can guarantee the results we seek. As a matter of fact, approaching wisdom in this manner is most likely a veiled attempt to control beyond our ability and authority—maybe even an attempt to control God. Many times God brings his leaders to places where he reminds them that the results are in his hands, not theirs. This can be especially true when working with staff. Godly leaders try to make the wisest choices possible with the available information and within their actual context, even though they cannot be certain of the outcome. Such is the central faith element of biblical wisdom and leadership.

Also remember that prayer is not a sidebar to leading or serving on a team. Rather, it is the core function for all leaders who desire to honor God with their leadership. I've committed myself to a regular practice of getting to my office early at least three times a week with the goal of spending that first hour (at least) reading Scripture, journaling, praying, and listening. I encourage you to find a way to consistently practice the spiritual disciplines that strengthen your spirit and your ability to hear the voice of God.

In later chapters, I break from the standard chapter format in order to explore other staff matters:

- In chapter 15 I discuss general principles that I consider when dealing with most staff challenges. Again, you must carefully and prayerfully consider how you should or can apply these principles to your challenges.

- In chapter 16 I offer some suggestions for creating a culture where staff are consistently appreciated and encouraged. You'll note that I use the metaphor of establishing a positive and encouraging "bedside manner." Your diligence in building and maintaining a positive and appreciative environment can inoculate your organization from many of these staff illnesses.

- While most chapters contain principles that are applicable to both paid and unpaid staff, in chapter 17 I will explain some key similarities and differences between them.

Proactive efforts to keep staff challenges from occurring in the first place require far less work than the time and energy needed to fix staff situations that have gone wrong. Remember that we're all human; no leader can prohibit all staff problems. They *will* occur. Wise and careful hiring or recruiting is one of the most important ways to head off staff problems. Enter the hiring or recruiting process intentionally and slowly, listening with all your mind, heart, and soul. Listening to the facts *and* your intuition is critical at these times. Don't be afraid to slow down the interviewing process considerably if your gut tells you to hesitate and be wary. Carefully explore these hunches and seek wise counsel from trusted friends whenever necessary.

I'd like to thank two people for their contributions to this book: First, Carolyn and I have been enjoying our life partnership for over thirty-five years. She's the delight of my life, and I love her now more than ever. In addition to contributing to the book several stories from her experience, she has assisted me on numerous occasions with her proofreading, editing, and "reality checks." (The diagnosis and treatment suggestions are still entirely from my experience and training, however.) Carolyn's prayers, listening ear, and godly counsel have significantly contributed to any success I have experienced in leading staff.

Second, Polly Lott and I have served together in various capacities and in two different institutions for almost twelve years now. I value her insightful advice and clarifying thoughts. Her input and stories have been invaluable to this book. What a wonderful privilege for my son Robb to also know Polly as his wife's mom! Yes, I'll admit it's a unique dynamic to serve together with my son's mother-in-law. The only major dilemma we've encountered is that when our first grandchild visits our office complex, it's a mad frenzy to see who'll get to hold Tucker first. Always the overachiever, I usually beat Polly to the task!

Finally, my prayer and hope is that my years of serving with staff may be of assistance to you in whatever role you hold—whether a staff member or leader of staff. Nothing is more exhilarating than being part of a team that serves with unity of purpose, passion, values, and vision. I've enjoyed that sense of exhilaration in many situations throughout the years, so I give my heartfelt thanks to all the staff with whom I've shared that privilege. I may have enjoyed serving with some of you more than others (forgive me if I let that show!), but I've tried to serve *all* of you with honor and respect, seeking to empower you to reach your full potential within God's kingdom. To *him* be the glory and praise.

1

Temporary Paralysis

Symptom: widespread inability to make decisions

This illness demonstrates itself through a persistent inability to make decisions on a personal or team level. Focusing too much on ensuring that everyone feels good about themselves, their place in the organization, and the process, results in the decision itself taking center stage to the exclusion of the effectiveness or wisdom of the decision—and what is ultimately best for the organization. Taking too much time to reach a decision and/or circling back to issues already thoroughly examined in the decision-making process are additional signs of this illness. The inability of other staff members to confidently know when a decision has been made signals that this illness needs thorough treatment.

"May I take some time to think about this decision and then get back to you?"

That sounds like a reasonable request, doesn't it? In fact, it sounds like a downright responsible request, signifying someone who does not take the role of decision maker lightly. Obviously when we have entrusted a staff member with responsibilities that involve risk taking and decision making, we want him or her to weigh risks, seek wisdom from others, and think carefully before making the choice. Sometimes, though, a well-intentioned staff member may become bound by the "paralysis of analysis"—unable to ever make a decision due to over-analyzing it!

This was the case with Harry, a pastoral staff member who continually sought to be trusted with growing levels of responsibility. But Harry seemed to believe that there was hardly a decision that would not be easier to make if put off till tomorrow, next week, or next year. Whatever the issue, he researched, asked opinions, mulled it over, sought more advice, typed out pros and cons, and then talked them over with his associates. And more often than not, he returned to square one without having made any progress at all—except notebooks full of lists of possible solutions!

Sadly, Harry carried his paralysis right into his style of leading a team. Harry was strong in helping his team talk about the challenges they faced, but when someone was ready to step up and move forward with a plan, Harry passed on his contagious paralysis by saying, "Before we take that step, why don't you take a little more time and perhaps write a memo for me that lists all the possible solutions and their consequences?" One of his staff reported that in three years of attending monthly team meetings under Harry's guidance, he had never once seen Harry make a decision or even delegate one to someone else!

Harry's disease had two unfortunate outcomes for his team: He tended to attract those who wanted to share his state of constant, consuming analysis, and he repelled those who had a thirst for progress and action.

Cataloging the Signs of Illness

1. Recurring inability to make decisions

Persons suffering from this illness appear unable to reach a decision and stay with it. Or they may fail to understand how to identify the variables that show a decision needs altering versus staying the course because the opposition or challenges to their decisions are simply a natural part of any decision. Sometimes the cause is fear of failure; other times it is an excessive need to be liked. Fear of conflict or risk taking may also contribute to this disease.

2. Too much attention to the decision-making process and how people feel about themselves, the team, and the leader

To my utter amazement, a lay leader once said to me, "The process is always more important than the outcome." Other leaders suggest that the outcome is more important than the process. Many dying organizations pride themselves on their strong process, but careful examination shows they fail to make good decisions. Paying proper attention to *both* aspects of decision making remains critical to the faithful completion of an organization's mission. This disease of temporary paralysis involves too much attention to the process, which produces the inability to reach decisions; this ultimately paralyzes the organization, placing it on a slow path to ineffectiveness and death.

3. Inability to convey to the staff when decisions are made or altering decisions so frequently that the staff get discouraged

One staff team I know is led by a pastor who can effectively rally her team to give an all-out effort to attempt seemingly impossible tasks. She knows how to get the most from the team she leads. However, she repeatedly and without warning changes the impossible task that she wants the team to accomplish. So she has to replace staff members far too frequently because they become exhausted or discouraged and then leave. The staff feel like they're being asked to climb a steep mountain, and suddenly, in the midst of the most exhausting part of the climb, they're asked to jump over to the bottom of another mountain and start all over. One staff member explained it this way: "So what hill does she want us to die on today and what will be the hill tomorrow?"

Certainly we must sometimes revise our decisions; we can only make decisions based on the Bible, prayer, and the best information before us. Sometimes as we implement a decision more facts become clear or situations change, requiring us to alter our choices. Revising decisions is not the issue. But making wholesale changes in direction too frequently or rapidly are signs of this illness.

4. Frequent retreating from decisions due to conflict and resistance

We all wish others would respond favorably to the decisions we make. This rarely occurred in the Bible, and unfortunately, unanimous support for our decisions will be rare in today's world too. Conflict and resistance will result from most decisions we make, no matter how obvious or wise the decision seems. Remember that Christians Against Almost Anything New (CAAAN) is an informal, international group that infiltrates most Christian organizations. This illness usually results from giving too much attention to the "no" votes and not focusing enough on those who *are* supporting the decision. Fear of conflict and an overactive need to be liked can also be contributing factors to this disease.

Treatment

Begin by giving staff members the benefit of the doubt and assuming that they have never been taught how to make effective decisions. I meet with staff members in a comfortable, warm setting and ask probing questions about their decision making. I start the conversation by asking how they are generally feeling about a pending decision. From this point I try to launch into questions about the process the staff member is using to reach a decision; in this way I attempt to uncover any feelings of fear or other reasons for indecisiveness. At the suitable moment, I ask if they would like some suggestions for improving the process and reducing the stress of decision making. Sometimes I encourage reading a helpful book or attending a seminar on decision making. Other times I ask if they would like some coaching on how to make good decisions, and together we develop a process for this mentoring to occur. This may include my attending team meetings to observe and then making suggestions for improvement. Or I might offer to meet one-on-one with the person as the need arises. When trust has been established, many times the staff members will initiate a more meaningful conversation on some of the deep-seated issues that have contributed to their indecisiveness. I listen carefully and offer suggestions for improvement.

Analyzing the culture of your organization may prove insightful when treating this illness. Does your culture allow failure and risk taking? Do you only implement changes where you can guarantee success? Do you celebrate and reward only successes? How about an award for the best attempt to succeed that actually failed? Do the senior leaders of the staff talk openly about their failures and successes? Can the staff humorously and kindly laugh at their mistakes? Does your staff consist mostly of overachieving stars?

Many times the reason a staff member can't make decisions is because the culture responds harshly to those who fail. Or the problem might lie in a culture where the decisions are made only by a select few. At one ministry where I served, staff were accustomed to asking the executive pastor to make all decisions they faced. Unfortunately, the executive pastor reinforced this harmful behavior because it made him feel needed. What a terrible shock when the new executive pastor (me!) refused to make any decisions that staff members should make for themselves. After many months, numerous conversations, and other affirmations, the staff discovered that they *could* make effective decisions.

Provide spiritual counsel to staff members who suffer from this paralysis. A local pastor here in the Denver area once jokingly told me that he intended to buy a Labrador retriever because he needed the kind of affection and affirmation that only a loyal pet could provide! All of us want to feel good about ourselves and our contribution to the organization where we serve and to be affirmed and liked. At times, though, we lose sight of the spiritual understanding that we serve out of the deep love relationship we have with the heavenly Father. We are affirmed and valued by him. Grasping this unconditional and complete love provides the most significant basis for our worth and service. We serve not to gain our heavenly Father's affection—we have that completely already—but to say *thank you* and to demonstrate our love for him. When he asks us to serve in difficult places, realizing this deep truth provides the only foundation for effective and faithful service.

Help staff members understand the meaning of consensus. Many times this paralysis results from misunderstanding consensus—which is one hundred percent *support* versus one hundred percent *agreement*. Consensus is the commitment to adequately listen to all viewpoints; once the decision is made by an appropriate majority of team members, then all members agree to fully support the team's decision. Church committee members notoriously violate this form of consensus. Helping staff members understand this and lead their teams to seek consensus rather than one hundred percent agreement may provide help for overcoming this illness. Personally modeling this before other staff members is the most effective way to communicate this important point.

Model and promote healthy conflict. Can we all agree that sometimes we just don't get a decision right and conflict can sometimes help us gain a better perspective and reach a wiser decision? Healthy conflict that promotes effective listening, compassion, prayer, personal dignity, and deeper reflection actually *strengthens* our organizations. Distinguishing between healthy and destructive conflict enables us to determine the correct course of action to take when conflict occurs. With healthy conflict, you listen more, reflect more, talk more, and together find a method to move ahead. Unhealthy conflict usually has nothing to do with the actual decision or process. So trying to convince someone on the merits of the decision is not productive and may actually intensify the conflict.

Unhealthy conflict is generally personal in nature and includes sinful behavior. Biblical confrontation, repentance, and forgiveness are required to deal with this type of conflict. It takes courage and a strong team to address unhealthy conflict.

I have made some impressively bad decisions, especially when I was younger and less experienced. One that vividly stands out was my decision that a small group should multiply and grow into two small groups so more outsiders could be invited to join the two new groups. Who can argue against growth and including others? Another key rationale for my decision was that numerous strong leaders attended this small group. So I naively went to one of their small group meetings and explained to them how I wanted them to break into two groups. I then gave them a list of people waiting to join one of the newly formed small groups. The reaction was immediate and intense: *absolutely not*. They were not going to multiply and would hear no further reasons from me on how it would help the church. They were a closed group and fully committed to staying that way. Needless to say, I drove home that night a wiser, though discouraged, person. To push or attempt to force that small group of gifted leaders to split would have been fatal to my continuance on that staff.

At times, once a decision is made, the team and the leader must revise the decision as needed—but still stay the course. The difference between the previous story and this point centers on how important the change is to the health of the organization and the level of support for the decision. If the decision is urgent and vital to the continued health of the organization, staying the course is necessary. Always count the "yes" votes and analyze who is saying no and why. Respectfully address the rationale of those resisting. While we need to listen carefully to why people are resisting decisions and respectfully respond, we should spend more time and energy on gaining support from those who can be influenced and reinforcing the support of those who are already on board. I try to model this and coach other staff members in this leadership approach. Try to build early momentum for your decision and tell emotionally moving success stories that reinforce the decision; at the same time, honestly address those things that are not going well, explaining how you will correct those. Watch to see if more people are getting on board or withdrawing their support. Encouraging your team to list possible reasons for resistance to a decision helps everyone better prepare for opposition.

Sometimes staff members suffer from this disease because they are in the wrong position and need to be reassigned within your organization or to another organization. Fred was an example of someone for whom this treatment worked. He was one of the most gifted "people persons" I have ever encountered. Yet his responsibilities on staff were 90 percent administrative. It didn't take a genius to see that Fred needed a position where he spent the majority of his time with people and little with administration. You also would expect Fred to welcome this change when I recommended it. No such luck. He resisted me for months. I decided to pray regularly and to build trust in our relationship. About six months later, he came to me and offered his resignation because he was so frustrated with his job. When we discussed how he might assume a different role at the church—one mostly focused on ministering directly to people—he reluctantly agreed. Six months later, he was one of the most effective people on our staff. And by the way, he never told me that he should've agreed to this rearrangement six months earlier!

At times this inability to make decisions may be deeply seated in the psyche of the staff member, requiring profes-

sional counseling. Please follow the suggestions for dealing with this form of treatment as described in chapter 8, "Lack of Large Motor Coordination."

A Final Word

An inability to make decisions paralyzes an organization and discourages other staff members. Allowed to worsen and expand, this illness may result in your best staff becoming discouraged and leaving. And ironically, you'll start *attracting* other staff who suffer from the same illness! Many times the organizational culture can create this illness, and treatment requires both individual and community focus.

2

Permanent Dilation
of the Pupils

Symptom: an extravagant taste for the spectacular and
most expensive

This illness includes an addictive thirst for spending
more and building ever bigger and with more magnifi-
cence each year. It is usually accompanied by a myopic
approach to one particular ministry as the single most
important in the church. The patients who lead the ministry may also exhibit signs of insecurity and confusion
over how to separate themselves and their worth from
these accomplishments. When diagnosing, you may be
wise to analyze the entire culture of the church. Ask
yourself, "Does the culture of our ministry actually reinforce this disease?"

Major Signs of Illness

The yearly Christmas extravaganza (the mere word *program* does not suffice) had grown to gigantic proportions. No longer a week's worth of concerts, it had expanded to nearly two full weeks—or a total of fifteen performances, counting two on each Saturday and Sunday and the dress rehearsal on the Thursday before. Design and preparations began a year ahead, and rehearsals started in July. Maybe that's what advertisers mean by "Christmas in July"?

The participants included set builders, directors, choir members, dramatists, sound and lighting engineers, seamstresses, makeup artists, ushers, parking lot attendants, cooks, kitchen helpers, aerial flyers, and elephant handlers—well, probably not the last two, but it certainly felt that way. They were told to schedule their entire holiday season around THE CHRISTMAS OUTREACH. Yes, it absolutely had the all-caps emphasis, with a bit of guilt usually thrown in as the final punctuation.

But it wasn't only the number of performances and participants that made the annual ritual so spectacular. By the time we moved on to another ministry, the "Living Christmas Tree," as it was affectionately called, could have qualified for its own zip code. It was a monstrosity of a skeleton (which could hold approximately seventy-five singers, depending on how much we choir members had eaten for Thanksgiving) built of wood, steel, screws, and a prayer or two, rising nearly fifty feet from floor to ceiling.

Once the builders were done, the tree needed to be stuffed, but *never* with fake pine branches. Oh no, for authenticity we went out into the countryside to cut at least one million branches. After that chore, two million twinkling lights were carefully placed.

And by carefully I mean *"The red light in quadrant five needs to move two inches to the left!"* sort of arranging. Choir members donned green robes (to match the pine, naturally) with tinsel around their necks. The lucky gal or guy who ended up at the top by the star was advised to buy more life insurance before the first performance.

But the tree was only one ring in the circus. By the time the children's choir; the dramatists (including live animals, which created a circus of sorts by themselves); the technology of lighted, specially designed backdrops; and the orchestra were all added in, quite frankly, there just weren't that many people left in the community to *watch* the performance.

And then came the final kicker: though more had been added this year, the music pastor would plead that next year just *had* to be even bigger and better and more creative! So, by the way, could we increase the budget just a tad? Say . . . by a hundred thousand or two?

The elephants were nearly a steal at one for five thousand or two for nine.

Cataloging the Signs of Illness

1. Extravagant taste for the spectacular and most expensive

You know you are in trouble when each year the budget continues to increase exponentially, with the activities becoming more breathtaking and dazzling, with little concern for strategic outcome. Why is it that in my church experiences the worship and youth staff members seem most prone to this illness?

2. Increased demands for a larger percentage of the church budget

If you are dramatically reducing the budgets of other significant ministry areas because this one ministry requires an exorbitant amount of monies to fund its programs, then you are suffering from this disease. Annual overspending and emotionally charged pleas with threats that "the church will suffer enormous harm if I (the ministry leader) can't have all the funds I've requested!" are other signs of potentially fatal symptoms.

3. Myopic understanding of the importance of one's ministry

A leader's reluctance to sacrifice any element of their dreams or plans for their ministry area for the sake of the whole church is another symptom of this disease. The inability to understand that "my ministry area exists to enhance the overall mission of the church" versus "the church exists as a platform to feature my ministry" usually accompanies this illness.

4. Total denial of the problem

Why can't we simply understand and accept ourselves as we are? That's probably a topic for another entire book, but the problem is evident here. When confronted with this illness, the patient will deny all wrongdoing and usually respond with impassioned justification. These ministry leaders tend to take even gentle confrontations as personal attacks, interpreting your concerns as evidence you do not believe in them or are not supporting their ministry area. Many times after a confrontation takes place, the senior leader will receive a call from a significant lay leader or donor inquiring about what is going on.

5. *Failure to meet budgetary parameters, often caused by a lack of training or giftedness*

When approaching this illness, carefully examine whether the real problem is a lack of training or giftedness. Sometimes the solution involves coaching or providing assistance from another person who can help manage the financial side. The key to this approach lies in finding a suitable financial helper to assist the highly creative artist-type leader. Select a helper who loves the ministry area and the leader, yet understands and appreciates the importance of treating this illness.

6. *Preferential treatment and accountability*

When other staff start testing the system ("Can we get a bigger slice of the pie too?") to see who gets preferential treatment and whether accountability is necessary, your church may be ready for the emergency room or lifesaving surgery. Nothing damages morale more than the perception that some staff or ministries are given preferential treatment because they are "special." This symptom requires immediate and thorough treatment. Whenever possible, a preventive, proactive system usually turns out to be the best approach.

Treatment

First, accurately discern where this ministry area fits into the overall scheme and mission of the church. Is the ministry leader correct in his or her assertion that the church will suffer if requested budget levels are not allocated? In light of the ministry's importance and its effect on the church's health, should you approach this quickly or over a longer period, trying a more indirect solution? Is this overspending starting to negatively impact other staff and the overall health of the church? While important, is it urgent that you act immediately or can you implement a more prolonged approach to solving the illness?

Assess the political nature of treating this illness. In one church where I served, the Christmas program was perceived by community members as one of the most important community events of the year, attracting over twelve thousand people annually. Tickets to these concerts sold faster than those for most sports events and touring rock groups. Therefore, gaining control over the spending of this annual event took time, careful skill, and correct timing. The worship leader had significant political clout in the church and in the community at large. Attempts to resolve the illness meant I was taking on an icon of the church. It needed to be done—but *very* wisely.

Listen carefully. When discussing this problem with the staff member, listen carefully, seek to understand his or her concerns, and affirm when appropriate. Express that your goal is to support this ministry area and leader in a way that ensures the mission of the church is fulfilled.

Consider the value of including a trusted third party in the discussions, especially if other meetings were not well received or were misunderstood. Intense, politically charged settings may also indicate you would be wise to involve a third party.

When meeting with the staff person for the first time, briefly explain the problem as you understand it; then ask the staff person to analyze the problem and its causes from his or her perspective. Listen for ways to build upon his or her analysis with some of your findings. Look for points of agreement as platforms from which to dive into the differences. Next, ask the leader for his or her possible solutions. Have the necessary factual information at hand—information like the budget versus actual expense figures from the past five years or so. An itemized list of expenses in that area may help also. If you have objective data that confirms that the event spends more than its outcomes warrant, that data could prove useful. The Christmas concerts at the church where I served were designed as evangelistic opportunities, yet the data clearly demonstrated that people were not coming to Christ; in actuality, church members were bringing their Christian friends rather than nonbelievers. This fact was helpful but not enough in itself since another goal of the concerts was building goodwill in the community. Some key questions to ask include, "How much must you spend to build goodwill among the community?" "Are there other, more strategic ways to use these funds to establish goodwill?"

Be ready to ask some probing but not attacking questions about certain expenses. Replace *why* questions (which could make the ministry leader defensive) with *how* questions such as, "How could we ensure that we meet the expectations and purpose of the event or program with alternative spending approaches?" and "Would recruiting a lay leader to serve as the financial liaison assist in managing expenses?" (More on this latter idea later.)

Evaluate if other methods might be suitable to fund the event. Ask questions such as, "Should we sell tickets or take an offering to fund the event?" or "Should we approach a couple of donors to fund the event as their ministry?" Be careful when approaching donors that you do not divert funds from the general church programs to this particular ministry. Another danger is that you might subconsciously encourage donors to over-fund this ministry and under-fund others. Therefore, I generally do not encourage this approach, although it may be a workable solution in some situations.

If you determine that the problem is lack of training, coaching, or giftedness, select some appropriate next steps. If training is needed, ask the ministry leader to research and identify some experiences that might be helpful. Provide the funds necessary for the training, but be prepared for the ministry leader to select the most expensive programs available! Do some advance research yourself for possible alternatives. Consider whether the funding of this training should be included in the ministry area's budget as a way to build accountability. The first time you implement this approach, it is probably wise to increase the budget.

If a lack of giftedness is the issue, help the ministry leader to select a person to assume responsibility for managing expenses—someone who has the expertise and is trusted by the leader. Unpaid staff might be willing to assist in these ways. Together, carefully select the volunteer and then explain the clear, expected outcomes plus the process for resolving conflict when it occurs. Do not establish a triangle between you, the ministry leader, and the lay leader. The lay leader usually needs to report to the ministry leader and should not attempt to do an "end run" around the ministry leader. However, you and the ministry leader *do* need to negotiate the appropriate means for appeal.

Keep the staff member responsible for developing and implementing appropriate solutions. Even when using a lay leader to assist, you need to clearly explain that the ministry leader retains ultimate responsibility for solving the problem.

Document all meetings and agreed-upon strategies, sending copies to the staff member and asking if your notes accurately reflect his or her understanding of the meetings. Keep all responses and make any changes as appropriate. Be clear about objective outcomes and measurements that you agree upon.

Insist on periodic accountability while staying appropriately flexible. Fully implementing this change will take time. The goal here is to meet periodically in an effort to prevent future problems from occurring. Make the accountability reachable, measurable, and specific, and place the responsibility for these meetings on the shoulders of the staff person. Require the staff person to come prepared to discuss both successes and failures and any corrective measures needed.

Love enough to insist that the offending staff member make the agreed-upon corrections. Flexibility is valuable, but allowing reoccurring problems to develop is not loving or wise. A tough love approach includes clearly stating that if the ministry leader overspends his or her budget this year, next year's budget will be automatically reduced to reflect that overspending. Use this type of tough approach sparingly and only when necessary.

After repeated attempts to solve the problem, replacing the staff member may be necessary if he or she simply refuses to get spending under control. However, this is a last resort. Before starting down this path, ensure that you have the necessary political clout, authority, and supervisory support; have followed a thorough process; have good documentation; can state the problem in a clear manner; and have a transitional plan in place. Never begin the process of removing staff without the full support of the appropriate authorities in your church setting. And no matter how fully prepared you might be, I guarantee that taking this path will be messy, requiring enormous amounts of emotional, physical, and spiritual energy.

A Final Word

Allowing one staff person or ministry area to repeatedly overspend damages morale and can negatively affect your institution's overall effectiveness and health. Unfortunately, this disease usually involves one of your most gifted staff members; therefore, dealing with the challenge will consume a tremendous amount of your time and energy. Sacrificing the church's overall health or your leadership effectiveness due to fears that you might lose the gifted staff member or cause conflict will not produce peace. Remember, "peace at all costs" is a misnomer; in reality, you will only produce *more* conflict.

3

Stiff Neck

Symptom: "ownership" of a specific church program

This illness involves leaders viewing any church program as their possession in need of protection—such as vacation Bible school, visitation night, or other long-standing traditions, usually including several nonnegotiables carried over from the last century. These could include insisting that vacation Bible school *must* be five days long and last four hours each day and must include easily misunderstood choruses (*Hide a light under a what? And where in the world is Sunshine Mountain?*) or other activities which make guests or church members feel uncomfortable.

Major Signs of Illness

A friend of ours was telling our small group that she had decided she was *not* going to work at our church's

VBS that summer. She'd been manipulated and guilted into volunteering for too many years, and she simply didn't have the time or energy for the two-week commitment that it required. Therefore, she had determined to say no in a mature, dignified way—to the leader's face. That very morning, she told us, she'd seen Ms. VBS in the grocery store. Gathering all her courage and strength of character, she then proceeded to *crouch down behind the apple display in the produce aisle and slink out of the store undetected!*

Cowardly? Indeed it was, our friend readily admitted with a laugh. But the point is this: when your faithful and committed volunteers from previous years (which she indeed had been) resort to hiding in the produce aisle, that's a sign you're in desperate need of change!

Cataloging the Signs of Illness

1. Volunteers bail out

As indicated in the story above, you're in serious trouble when your volunteers are making excuses, failing to show up when they've agreed to, or (creatively) avoiding your leaders during recruiting periods. Even your most dedicated helpers grow weary of tired, possibly out-of-date, and repetitive programs. One church's "Visitation Nights" program started with an army but dwindled to a faithful few—and those attended mostly because a hot dog supper was provided to keep it alive!

2. Decreasing attendance

Granted, numbers are not always a sign of success, nor are they the only guarantee of success. (Defining "success" in ministry is a discussion for another time!)

But these warning signs should not be ignored. You also need to evaluate the numbers themselves: Who makes up those you're attempting to serve? Is the growth (or stagnation) merely among Christian attendees? Are you merely ministering to the same group year after year? And if you are specifically targeting the unchurched, are you seeing those people reflected in the head count?

3. Lack of participation by the unchurched community

No church can afford to instantly or automatically disregard the "latest and greatest" which could possibly inject new life into a stagnant church; "seeker-oriented" or "seeker-sensitive" ministries were a spark for many in the past. At the same time, we cannot cater to the community to the detriment of the body's need for Christian formation. It's a tricky tightrope that we walk to balance reaching out to the unsaved with ministering to the growth of our members, for that is definitely God's desire for the church. This is not an either-or situation; overall, we should be serving *both* Christians and the unchurched.

Most of all, our evaluation of ministries must stay attuned to following God's heart and agenda—not ours! Are we using God's resources for his heart and mission for the church? This is not about our agenda, our desires, our pet projects. Instead, we must follow God's plan, which is to reach the world for Christ.

4. General sense of tiredness

This one's tougher to define. But to get at this more ethereal symptom, here are questions you can ask your team from the previous year:

- Does this program feel worn out?
- Do you feel worn out?

- Has this program served its purpose in the past . . . and now we need to move on to something new?
- Do you sense that we're still making a difference in lives?
- Does it feel like this is a 1940s program . . . for a 2000s world?
- Are you excited about starting up this year?
- Are others sending us direct or indirect signals that changes are needed?

5. Unbending leadership

Now we're getting to the heart of the problem. If you've discovered that all the other symptoms are profoundly demonstrated, and yet your leader won't adapt, change, or be open to a totally new direction, then you're in serious need of treatment. Take two aspirin and call your leader's doctor in the morning. (Don't you wish that would work?)

One church's pre-marriage class, which had been practical and successful for years, was in dire need of revamping. Though it had worked well in the past, the twelve-week class attendance requirement proved difficult for full-time, dual-income couples and nearly impossible for those who lived out of town. The program director refused to acknowledge that we now live in a more diverse and mobile society. Therefore, to the complete frustration of future brides and grooms who sincerely desired to complete the pre-marriage program, he demonstrated no willingness to accommodate their very reasonable needs. The reality: culture has changed. Without sacrificing theologically in any way, the program desperately needed to adapt and change as well.

At an educational institution where I served, pancake breakfasts on Saturday mornings had become a yearly tradition to reach out to alumni. At one time attendance ran around one hundred, a good number for that type of ministry. But when numbers dwindled to less than twenty—since parents now either jealously protect their time with children on the weekends or are busy running to an activity—it was time to find another mode of outreach.

Treatment

Respectfully and honestly evaluate ministries, personnel, and those being served by ministries with criteria for effectiveness you've established in advance. You might want to consider asking questions like: Are these ministries meeting those criteria? Are they still effective? Are they reaching for God's heart for the church—to minister to believers and the unchurched? Is this the best way to honor God and be wise stewards of the resources which God has given us? This assessment is healthy for churches and parachurch organizations and should be done on a regular basis—not merely in times of crisis.

The most important evaluation may take place as you analyze yourself: "What are my true motives for desiring change? Is this mindless change (for the sake of being different) or change merely to heal my personal boredom?" You need to ask yourself, "Is my heart aligned to God's heart and what he desires?"

For those ministries that appear to need changes, can you work with the current directors to make substantial modifications? Are those people able to change? Seek confidential advice from a trusted supervisor or other staff member on how he or she assesses the possibility of this person changing.

If you determine that the leader can change, meet with him or her in a comfortable setting. Listen carefully to diagnose the real issues that you face in this situation, and ask him or her to make a specific list of what changes will be made and how they will be handled. Document these strategies and include accountability mechanisms or checkpoints.

Following your meeting, send a copy of these strategies to the person, asking if you have accurately captured the details of the meeting. Document any response to your written summary. Remember to keep the *leader* responsible for the changes. You serve as the coach and cheerleader. Be careful to not allow the leader to manipulate you into assuming responsibility for making the changes or this could backfire into allegations of interference.

If you make the determination that you must replace the director, an honest confrontation in your office is essential. Before this can take place, you must make sure that:

1. *The timing is correct.* Allow enough time to implement your transitional plan so that you are not in crisis mode.
2. *All documentation is in place.*
3. *The appropriate pastoral staff and elders have been informed and are in agreement, if necessary.* Ask yourself, "Will they stand firmly with me in the face of resulting conflict?"
4. *Your transitional plan has been designed and is ready to put into place.* You must have thought through who will take over the leadership, how you will announce this change, and whether you will eliminate the program or replace it with a new one.
5. *You've thoroughly evaluated the fallout.* For example, who else is directly aligned with this staff member or volunteer leader and will be hurt or affected

by his or her release? These people may need to be appropriately informed; therefore, establish a means of communicating the change to all those involved while maintaining confidentiality.

6. *You're prepared to handle this in a loving and yet professional manner.*

7. *You have decided whether you should invite a trusted third party to participate in the confrontation.*

8. *You thank this leader in an appropriate way.* For example, is a retirement celebration called for?

A Final Word

Everyone knows that by itself, a stiff neck is not fatal. But attempt to drive a car, play with your children, or work in your garden, and you'll note how this disability seriously hinders your movements. Allow that to happen too often in your church or ministry, and it won't be able to move either—except backward.

4

Swollen Brain

Symptom: a firm belief that "I pretty much know it all already"

Staff members suffering from this illness tend to be more experienced in ministry and have had past success in leading ministry using approaches that are now dated. No longer interested in new ideas, quite confident from their past success, and fully convinced they are experts in ministry, they tend to have stopped growing or adapting. They view newer forms of ministry as passing fads or unnecessary accommodations to present culture or weak Christians—although sometimes they are correct in their assessments. More than once I have listened to their diatribes on how "they just don't make Christians the way they used to." Many times gender issues can be a significant aspect of this disease. Obvious or more subtle forms of condescension typically accompany this malady as well.

Major Signs of Illness

Bill was a widely respected pastor, particularly well liked by the seniors to whom he ministered with a protective kindness. His homespun charm, wisdom, and love for God and people made him a likable guy to serve with. That is, unless one disagreed with him. Bill didn't take well to being reined in or even questioned; he welcomed all opinions that *agreed* with his! When disagreements arose, he employed a defense method that worked more often than not: Bill simply responded in such a condescending manner that the respondent walked away, somewhat dazed, reconsidering why he or she had *dared* to raise the issue in the first place! His retorts varied from "Well, I believe I've been doing God's work long enough to know" to "I'm sure that sounds like a fine idea, but when you've been around as long as I have . . . !" More than once the fresh ideas of young pastors or even new believers were stopped in their tracks by Bill's defensive technique.

The female members of the staff often took the brunt of patronizing remarks veiled in kind and gentle tones ("Now listen here, *little lady*"), and some accepted this as a side of Bill that couldn't be changed. Others did not. When he directed one of the female administrative staff (one who did not report to him) to take on the responsibility of the daily organizing and straightening of a shared supply room "because that's what you ladies do so well," she was, not surprisingly, livid!

Cataloging the Signs of Illness

1. Good-hearted dinosaurs locked in memories of a past, nonexistent, golden age

Finding success in their past ministry efforts, leaders with this disease are unable to make the changes to appropriately relate to the emerging leaders of a new time. Bill—mentioned in this chapter's opening story—was well liked even though he frustrated so many of the women and younger staff. Even those he frustrated or angered the most accepted his good-natured spirit and warm personality. Everyone knew that if you needed something, Bill would be there to help if he could.

2. Operating mouth before brain is engaged

Some suffering from this malady lack necessary social skills or suffer from foot-in-mouth disease. When kindly confronted, they will seek forgiveness and try to improve. However, many will struggle with this issue for a lifetime.

3. Mean-spirited condescension

Some leaders can be mean-spirited and harsh in their condescending words and attitudes. These require more aggressive forms of treatment and isolation from healthy staff members. A staff member in a church where I served notoriously lived in a foul mood, caustically taking his bad attitudes out on others. Far too much energy was spent trying to fix the damage caused by his inconsiderate words. Unfortunately, I did not have the support needed to remove him from the staff. So we redesigned his office area and moved him into a back room, away from contact with most of the public and staff. Some of us took it upon ourselves to warn all new staff members how to deal with his tough-spirited persona. Yes, I hear what you are thinking. He should have been released. Sometimes the politics of the real world mean that you need to find a workable solution—even though it's definitely not the best solution. Remember, we are all under some form of authority or supervision.

4. Hidden insecurities

Ego issues and insecurities characterize many of the staff ill with this condition. Unable to cope with the risk and uncertainty of changes in culture or to gain new ministry skills, they find ways to deny reality and defend their lack of growth. Criticizing new ideas and approaches is a subtle form of hiding one's fear or the frightening realization that one doesn't quite measure up anymore. For example, one staff member I worked with could not type; she attempted to hide this inadequacy by being publicly critical of any technology. She would repeatedly point with pride to her "commitment to people versus technology" as the better way. The real problem was simply her fear of being discovered as not able to type.

5. The sin of pride

Pride combined with a high intellect can lead staff members to use a condescending style; they regard their skills too highly and view others as inferior or not to the level of their sophistication. Many times this type of pride is really a form of insecurity. Other times it is just plain sinful arrogance. Bart grew up in an upper-class family with all the privileges and rights of wealth. These privileges had opened doors for him into some of the finest educational institutions in the world. His tastes for clothes, food, hotels, and vacation spots, among other things, were outlandish by most standards. He expected to be acknowledged for his superiority and treated in a privileged fashion. Those of us coming from middle-class backgrounds were quickly and subtly—yet most definitely—informed of the superiority of his upbringing.

Treatment

Generally, a subtle, low-key approach to this illness is better than a direct assault. So, when facing one suffering with swollen brain, I try to diagnose which of the signs listed above best describes the situation I am facing. Is this person good-spirited or mean-spirited? How is pride or insecurity involved? Is the staff member older? Is this a matter of a blind spot in this person's life? If needed, seek the counsel of others who are wise and trustworthy to more fully diagnose what expression of this illness you are dealing with. Keep this as confidential as you can.

Design an approach suited to the situation. With Bill, I gently confronted him on his behavior and tried to provide some suggestions for how he could improve, while at the same time accepting the reality that comprehensive change was unlikely. My goal was to help him reach a more acceptable place. This required multiple gentle confrontations and much work on my part to ensure that when I talked with Bill, it wasn't just about his negative behavior. Building trust and providing positive affirmation were critical.

Coaching and positive affirmation are the best places to start, if possible. Once I recruited the assistance of another older staff member who had observed this same negative behavior. Since both staff members trusted each other and had a strong relationship, he willingly agreed to confront his friend and offer some suggestions for improvement.

This method actually strengthened their relationship, provided an accountability partner, and resulted in positive changes.

Mean-spirited forms of this illness require a more direct and formidable approach. Usually I do not meet with these folks alone. Instead, after completing the necessary documentation (which should always include date, time, location, witnesses, and a brief description of the behavior that was inappropriate), I solicit the assistance of another supervisor. Sometimes this includes the senior leader of the organization. I know that we all wish to appear to the senior leader as capable of handling these issues without bothering him or her; however, those with cruel forms of this disease tend to be skilled fighters and will quickly assume a fighting posture when confronted. Most times, after being confronted, those with this malady will go directly to the senior leader to accuse *you* of some form of wrongdoing. Be prepared for this massive attempt to deflect the conversation from their unsuitable behavior to you as the enemy. Many times it will be nearly "guerrilla warfare," including tactics like recruiting other influential, disgruntled staff members to join them in their fight. Or they may lie in wait, looking for mistakes you make in the future and bringing those to your and others' attention.

Usually treating this illness means a battle of the intellect to see who is the shrewdest and can out-maneuver the other. Stay out of any form of scheming and work to solve the problem; don't get caught up in subtle forms of distraction. You can prevent some of this by ensuring that your senior leader is fully informed and supportive of the efforts to correct this sickness. The more prepared and proactive you are with documentation of multiple instances and multiple witnesses, the better you can keep the focus on the staff member exhibiting this improper behavior. Try to be prepared for the fight without *predisposing* yourself for a fight.

Remember the underdog syndrome—others will rally to defend someone they think has been treated poorly. When dismissing staff members, treat them fairly and follow due process. Once I had received numerous and passionate complaints about the performance of a youth pastor. Parents were insistent that this staff member had to be replaced. Their criticisms were substantial, clearly organized, and well documented. I made a mistake in the way I handled the situation, and to my utter amazement, *the parents turned on me* and became the defender of this youth pastor—the very same one who, just weeks before, they had argued so passionately must be dismissed! Another time I watched as staff members—who were so vehement about the failures of another staff member—turned on their supervisor because they judged that she had not respectfully dealt with the problem. Church members and other staff members want all staff—even those they struggle with—to be treated fairly, with respect, and following due process; otherwise, they become concerned about how *they* might be treated if they ever faced that same situation. Be cautious and careful here!

When dealing with pride, try to center the conversation on appropriate and inappropriate behavior, not the pride. Some readers may think that I am not facing the real issue and should confront the sin. At times, that may be the right approach. However, my experience demonstrates that keeping the conversation on *behaviors* tends to prevent the person from feeling like I am attacking their value or worth as a person. If the person being confronted introduces the topic of their pride into the conversation, then I will gently allow the conversation to include a discussion of this sin. Sometimes the strength of your relationship with the other person allows you to address issues of pride. While I am deeply concerned about the issues that may be contributing to their condescending attitudes and I do need to diagnose those in order to prepare treatment, I try not to become their therapist—it just confuses the issues and boundaries. I know some of you are thinking that it's not about being their therapist; rather, it's about being their pastor. Again, I try to carefully diagnose the situation, seeking God's wisdom in how to best lead the person I am confronting. In your situation, you too must decide.

A Final Word

After reading this chapter, you might be tempted to ignore this illness or be afraid to attempt any treatments. Remember that no one enjoys conflict. We simply know that it is inevitable and must be wisely embraced and managed. Peace at all costs is too costly. Research has demonstrated that when people lose their jobs over conflict, it is because they *failed to address or admit that the conflict existed*. Leading in conflict-filled situations demands a lot of faith, wisdom, and determination. You must believe that God can and will guide you. He is trustworthy. Always be prayerfully seeking counsel, and be wise.

5

Underdeveloped Brain

Symptom: it's gotta be new to be good

This ailment refers to those who toss out anything that appears to be more than a year old. Expressions which you may often hear are "That's old school," "That isn't the newest way of doing things," "That isn't cutting edge," and even "Mosaic isn't doing that!" Frequent use of these phrases may be a reliable indicator of this disease. I once heard a speaker, writer, and national guru say, "You have to toss out all thinking from the past and replace it with brand-new thinking in order to effectively reach people in this generation." Are you thinking that I might be misquoting him? Unfortunately, not so, as I even verified his remarks by reviewing the DVD of his presentation.

The nuances of this illness aren't whether old approaches are inherently bad or new approaches are intrinsically good. This illness is about the inability to carefully determine which strategies are appropriate for effectively serving in the world and in the specific context where we minister. This can include wholesale dismissal of either the new or the old. Lack of prayerful reflection and a superficial understanding of key universal principles characterize this virus.

Major Signs of Illness

Staff leader Tammy seemed compelled to be viewed as a young, innovative leader who knew all the latest and greatest trends in her area of ministry. Repeatedly, I heard hushed yet audible groans from her team members when she announced that she was off to a new conference or was distributing another article on a new approach to their ministry area for discussion by her staff. Equally disturbing was the frequent distribution of the subsequent article that appeared in the next month's issue—now rebutting the ideas of the *previous* article. More than once I heard from staff, "Can't we wait to discuss this article until next month when we have the rebuttal too?" Perhaps because Tammy's last name was toward the end of the alphabet (or for other reasons I don't know), Tammy would receive her copies of the latest journals up to a week later than some of her friends. Therefore, she would go to the Internet and try to download the latest articles as soon as they were available. After all, how could she possibly not be the first to read and discuss the latest thoughts on ministry innovation?

I often wondered why she couldn't hear or see the signs that she was fatiguing her staff members. Yet not only did she miss those signs, but she also pressed ahead, fully convinced in her mind that the staff eagerly anticipated these times of exploring new ideas. Whenever her young staff assembled at their favorite coffee shop or

Diet Coke dispenser without Tammy, the conversation quickly turned to "When is she going to stop and allow us to actually implement an idea before she changes direction again?" On occasion I even had the opportunity to listen as she explained to her ministry peers outside of the church how much her staff was on board and ready to tackle all new challenges. I was aware that on numerous occasions, staff members had tried to communicate their displeasure, but Tammy merely attributed these concerns to the stress of being in the middle of a transitional stage of her ministry plans.

What a sad day when her staff collectively decided to use a confidential 360-degree performance review form to put in print what they had been trying to say to her for months. Tammy's first response was to attribute the honest and tough feedback to one disgruntled staff member. My challenge was to help Tammy face the fact that although her staff loved her, they needed her to recover from this addiction to being seen as "the most innovative leader" in her peer group.

Cataloging the Signs of Illness

1. Addiction to the latest, greatest idea or the flavor-of-the-month club

Fear that one might be perceived as "old school" or behind the times becomes a driving force for those suffering from this illness. A desire to appear to others as having only the most original ideas, ministries, or strategies compels these folks to reject any ideas that give an indication of being used elsewhere or coming from other sources. Just as ice cream shops often feature a unique flavor of ice cream during certain months, without a well-thought-through strategic framework for the ministries they lead, too many church leaders succumb to what sells or what seems most exciting this month. Giving constant attention to the newest ideas without careful reflection on the past or on the amount of change a group can handle usually indicates this illness.

2. Confusion about being gifted and passionate inventors or entrepreneurs

Although truly gifted inventors may suffer from this disease, this particular illness occurs more often in those who *do not* possess these skills but desire to give the impression that they *do*. Or it may describe those inventors/entrepreneurs who refuse to carefully understand how the contributions of the past and present inform their thinking for the future. Usually, however, these types of inventors/entrepreneurs are not very successful; they fail to recognize where they are in the stages of innovation and lack the ability to build upon the wise learning experiences of others. This is a key symptom: they tend to repeat the same mistakes of the past because they do not believe anything valuable comes from the past.

3. Lacking experience or maturity

Please hear me out on this point. I'm attempting to describe a common symptom, not come across as critical. Yes, those who are older can be set in their ways and closed to necessary innovation. The opposite is also sometimes true: younger leaders can easily dismiss the contributions and wisdom of those more experienced in ministry. Learning to discern and utilize wisdom from more experienced leaders can be a valuable skill which eliminates unnecessary mistakes and conflict. Numerous mature leaders in Christian organizations around the world are also young at heart—innovative and accepting of the value of change. My suggestion to young leaders is to ask one or two mature leaders to mentor you. Most of all, we must all be about the hard work of identifying those universal and timeless principles that define a biblical understanding of the church and its God-directed work.

4. Needing to reject the past to differentiate oneself

An inordinate need to differentiate oneself from others—merely for the sake of feeling good about one's self—may indicate the existence of this disease. In an almost adolescent manner, sometimes staff members reject anything that looks like or sounds like the past—simply because they are afraid they will lose their individual expression or become irrelevant. Other times I wonder if the issue is simply a failure to understand and honor the wisdom of the past. This disease can also emerge because the senior leaders fail to properly recognize, support, and encourage younger, emerging leaders. They may not be allowing these younger ones the freedom to explore alternative forms of ministry. When diagnosing this malady, exploring the full range of symptoms and causes will help in designing your treatment.

5. Addicted to change for change's sake

On those occasions when an organization or ministry needs to move out of a stalled state and into action, change for the sake of change alone can be an acceptable choice. When staff members implement mindless changes because of personal boredom, however, they probably suffer from this malady. That is the most distinguishing feature of this illness—implementing mindless change without regard for how it will positively or negatively affect a specific community or organization. My ministry experience has clearly shown that approaches that are workable in one geographical region will not necessarily work in another. I have also learned the importance of understanding and committing to the hard work that is necessary when you decide that major organizational change is required.

Treatment

The single most important approach in treating this illness is developing a biblically sound and wise strategic framework to guide the work of your institution. Many books can assist you in how to design this strategic framework for your church or ministry. Even if your senior leaders have not attempted this process for the entire organization, you can lead your team in understanding and defining the work and future for your part of the ministry. Go to Denver Seminary's webpage (www.denverseminary.edu/president/booklist) for a list of possible resources. Or go to the seminary's website and select the page on Denver Seminary's strategic framework to see a model of what I'm suggesting.

Stay away from the business plan approach; that usually means a lot of unnecessary work, ultimately producing a large manual that sits on a shelf and everyone soon forgets. Your goal is strategic thinking by all members of the staff (or the ones you lead). Once completed, this framework should be approximately eight to ten pages maximum, with many graphics and visual enhancements. Avoid lengthy paragraphs and discourses.

Using a healthy group process to gain input and build ownership enables all team members to feel affirmed and mobilized to implement the framework. All frameworks need annual discussion and revisions to ensure their effectiveness. However, frameworks still provide the road map for the work of your staff and help them to understand their part in the mission of your organization. Frameworks also serve as helpful screening instruments to evaluate the latest trends. Remember, the ultimate goal is to call your team or organization into a process for jointly listening for the voice of God, discerning his direction for your ministry, and implementing it. The framework is *not* designed to limit innovation or risk taking; rather, it provides parameters and focused discipline for all staff members, encouraging them to explore without demoralizing other staff.

If this illness occurs because senior leaders have created a culture that stifles the creativity of the innovators on staff, break that cycle. Feeling controlled, innovators tend to push back by automatically rejecting the values and ideas of the senior leaders. This produces even more attempts to control from the senior leaders, who now feel unappreciated or disrespected. So the cycle continues and just reinforces itself. It is up to the senior leaders to break this destructive cycle. Every Christian organization needs some level and form of research and development where risk taking is encouraged and expected. Young, emerging leaders need to gain the wisdom and confidence that comes from taking risks and implementing new ideas. Senior leaders need to encourage and support these innovators, which probably means they'll need to stretch beyond their own comfort levels, providing wise counsel when younger leaders may be overlooking some important facts.

Respect and trust those who serve with you, and you will receive respect and trust in return. Ask yourself, "Will what I'm about to do increase or destroy trust between myself and others?" During the numerous times when I have felt called to trust other staff members, I've said, "Well, I'm not fully comfortable with that approach, but I hear your rationale and heart. So let's find a way to implement some of these ideas without risking the health of the entire organization." Some of you may be thinking that you should never risk the future of the entire organization. Those times are indeed very infrequent and should be entered only because the leaders of the organization feel *compelled* by the Spirit of God to proceed in this manner—not because we need a new personal challenge.

When working with an individual staff member suffering from this disease, offer personal coaching or assist the staff member in recruiting another trusted person to provide coaching. By determining to think the best and give the benefit of the doubt, I usually choose to believe that suitable training is the answer. This is not always the solution, but it's a great place to start. Numerous seminars and resources can also provide training on how to develop a strategic framework for an organization or team. Within the organization's budget, I always work to ensure that adequate funds are available for ongoing professional development in this critical area.

A couple of times I found it necessary to form an agreement with the staff member that no new idea could be introduced to his or her staff without first convincing me that it was necessary. This served two purposes: First, it helped keep me up to speed on the latest thinking in a certain ministry area. Second, it provided discipline for the staff member in learning to carefully think through the motivation for introducing new ideas. My goal was to help without controlling or assuming responsibility for what the staff needed to do.

If necessary, help the person with this problem find a better placement within your organization or with another one. At times the problem may be chemistry or suitable placement within the organization. Bert was one of the most creative thinkers I have ever known. He could see things from perspectives that generally never crossed my mind. Maintaining the status quo or dealing with staff conflict or lack of productivity destroyed his spirit and motivation. When I first arrived at this particular organization, I quickly realized that he was not suited for the organization or the position where he served. My job? I needed to assist him in identifying that he didn't fit in that particular position and to help him find the courage he needed to trust God and make the change that we all knew he needed to make. Typically, he resisted most of my early attempts to help him decide to move to an organization that desperately needed his talents. After many hours of conversation, ample transitional time to secure a new ministry location, and a final push from me, he relocated to a new ministry which was designed for innovation. He has never been happier!

Another option when treating this malady is to help the person find other outlets for his or her need to innovate or discuss the latest ideas. Internet blogs or chat rooms filled with discussions of the latest trends may be a good choice. The point here is to find positive outlets to satisfy one's passion to participate in the conversations on the latest ideas in one's areas of interest.

Try not to blur together the professional relationships of reporting or serving by becoming someone's counselor. I try to offer biblically wise pastoral advice as requested and when appropriate, but if deep-seated personal issues are contributing to this illness, I encourage the staff person to seek outside professional help (as described in chapter 8) or the assistance of a trusted friend. Some of you may not agree with this advice, so you must decide after prayerfully seeking God's guidance.

A Final Word

When treating this illness, focus on how to bring disciplined habits to the staff member while still encouraging that person's beneficial gifts and contributions to the organization. The goal is to help those suffering from this disease find the wisdom of when and how to bring innovation to their staff or organization. Coaching them on the proper ways to judge an appropriate pace for change and innovation may also help. Above all, don't squelch this person's voice in your organization! Properly led, these innovators can guide us into healthy conversations—discussions which far too many organizations subconsciously work to ignore.

6

High Blood Pressure

Symptom: a belief in reaching people for Christ through
outrageous activities

Why do youth and worship staff tend to think so creatively and outside the realm of normalcy? Could it be in their God-given DNA? Stories abound of youth or worship staff members who push the edges of sensible behavior. I'm not talking about moral or ethical issues but extreme "out of the box" attempts to reach people for Christ. I'm sure you've heard some of those wild stories: riding motorcycles down the aisles and even up onto the platform; tossing Frisbees from the top of the piano or organ to people in the balcony; throwing watermelons—or televisions!—off the roof of a three-story educational building; or using ideas from a book called *The Dictionary of Grossology* (yes, that is the actual title; I'll leave it to your imagination to envision the types of activities suggested in *that* book!). All of these were good-spirited, well-intentioned attempts to reach others for Christ. But here's the good news *and* the bad news: they were indeed effective tools for evangelism, but they were also effective in bringing massive amounts of criticism for the senior leader!

Major Signs of Illness

It's hard to match the enthusiasm of an energetic youth pastor on a roll, isn't it? There's no doubt that we need these dedicated men and women who are passionate about reaching the next generation—and willing to risk whatever they must to do so, whether it be funds, facilities, or the perfunctory goodwill of the congregation. Of course, this malady is not limited only to youth pastors; anyone with great passion for the ministry can be afflicted. But the symptoms do tend to present themselves with greater frequency among those in youth ministry!

One friend told me of his own experience as a youth pastor when he and his team had planned a "western jamboree" for the junior highers in their Midwest town— a high-budget, high-impact event that they hoped would attract many unchurched teens. And a glorious event it was, with hay bales, cowboys (costumed youth leaders), a barbecue with all the trimmings, and even a pig borrowed from a church member's farm to be employed for the greased pig chase! The junior highers joined in with great excitement and brought their friends as planned, and clearly many new kids would be coming to the youth department and perhaps someday to Christ because of their initial participation in this hilarious, fun event. It was deemed a marvelous success.

Early the next morning—a Sunday—the youth pastor was still basking in the glory of a job well done when the phone rang. Before he managed to get the phone to his ear, he could already hear a nearly hysterical voice on the other end! Holding the phone at arm's length, he finally was able to decipher the raised voice as that of the facilities director, who clearly, judging by his tone, did *not* share the joy of this well-executed plan. What could possibly have provoked such fury? Well, when the youth pastor brought that full-grown hog from the farm to the event, perhaps he should have considered a more appropriate mode of transportation than the church van that was used every Sunday morning to pick up the elderly members! Even though some appreciable effort had been made to return the van to a clean condition, imagine the facility director's surprise when he unlocked the van's door and was hit with the unmistakable smell of fresh hog manure—not to mention the sight of the scuffs and deep scratches that a pent-up hog will inevitably make when trying to extricate himself from the confines of a church van! Needless to say, regrettably, there was never another western jamboree held for the junior highers in this church—and the youth pastor was fortunate to get off with just a one-hundred-decibel lecture.

Cataloging the Signs of Illness

1. Passionate dedication to reach people for Christ

How can anyone argue with this? I can't! The point isn't the passion or dedication. It is the inability to express these strengths within a proper range of decorum. When confronting this behavior, the typical response will be something like, "Don't you care about those who need Jesus?" The strong hint is that *any* controls upon their behavior are unreasonable and limit their effectiveness in sharing the gospel. Good motives usually accompany these crazy and riotous activities. If you come up against bad motives or harsh attitudes, you are probably identifying another form of this disease which will be examined later in this chapter.

2. Inability to see how one's actions can negatively affect others—especially when done for a good cause

How many harebrained ideas are justified because of good motives? Those with this illness exhibit the inability to move beyond their passion or creativity to take the time to analyze the possible results of their planned actions. Certainly youthfulness and inexperience can be factors in this malady. The fundamental issue is the failure to realize that good motives—no matter how noble—are not enough to justify an activity or action that fails to take into account the overall needs of the church or similar organization.

3. Lack of wisdom and unwillingness to listen or seek advice

This symptom can take on differing forms. In one instance it is simply not taking the time in advance or not seeing the value of seeking advice and listening. Another manifestation is just not having the life experience or being wise enough to evaluate how one's actions may negatively affect others. Deliberately overt or passive-aggressive refusal to listen and seek advice are other more fatal forms of this malady. Arrogance, stubbornness, rebellion, or overconfidence could contribute to this. An abnormal need for affirmation and recognition, usually expressed as insecurity, is yet another variety. The complementary illnesses of underdeveloped brain or permanent dilation of the pupils may also be intermingled with the various modes of this disorder.

4. An abnormal desire to prove one's ability or value

Here we are dealing with a problem that permeates one's sense of self-worth. Those suffering from this ailment want desperately to show others that they can be trusted and are worthy of leadership. Needing affirmation and recognition on an abnormal and insatiable level, they desire the freedom to express themselves in ways that are spectacular. They work to fix the emptiness inside themselves through external means. No matter how much they achieve or succeed, they will never find the healing they seek. Locked in an endless cycle that actually accelerates their addiction to achieve, they will push desperately, seeking what they can't reach because they're employing the wrong solutions.

Treatment

First you must diagnose the form of high blood pressure you're encountering. Are you dealing with inexperienced youthfulness? Or are you sensing rebellion, stubbornness, or arrogance? Could it be insecurity and an excessive need for affirmation? Generally I start with the diagnosis of inexperienced youthfulness, even if I think it may be one of the other forms of this malady. And, yes, many times it is a combination of all forms.

When treating inexperienced youthfulness, remember your own early years. I can't help but remember my own early years in ministry as a youth pastor. I have often said that as a senior leader I would have certainly fired myself for some of the stunts I pulled when I served as a youth pastor! What surprised me—and does so still—was all the support I received from the parents to continue with my antics. Evidently they saw the results in their teens, and therefore they trusted me to a level that amazed me. I am deeply indebted to Pastor Ralph Burns for his wise ability to corral my enthusiasm while empowering me to use my skills to engage youth for the cause of Christ. I will never know all the extra work he did and the personal price he paid behind the scenes to help the deacons see the value of what God was doing in the midst of these rowdy activities. Ralph, you are the best!

So now I do my best to coach and encourage those suffering from inexperienced youthfulness, remembering how Ralph invested in my life. Ralph always started our conversations with positive affirmations—bolstered by his numerous public affirmations of me. Then he would talk about how much he appreciated the way God was working in the youth ministry. The last part of our conversation usually went something like this: "Craig, in the future, when you plan an outrageous activity, please give me advance warning so I can help you accomplish your goals while ensuring that I can head off any criticisms that might come from others." Therefore, we made a pact. Within limits, I could continue to be crazy and wild in my approach to youth ministry, and he would provide the experience that I lacked in understanding the full ramifications of my ideas. It worked great! Yes, he had to tell me no at times, but usually he gave me advice on how to adapt my ideas in a way that accomplished my goals and resulted in less resistance.

Sometimes when treating inexperienced youthfulness, allowing the staff members to face the full consequences of their actions can prove beneficial. Ensure that the consequences are within acceptable parameters, and try to pick something that will require a lot of work from them to fix—but won't result in permanent damage to the ministry, the staff person, or you as leader. Throwing watermelons, televisions, and various other indescribable items off the roof of a three-story educational building is not what I would choose to do; however, it was firmly in the hearts of the youth staff as a great way to attract unchurched youth. So my agreement was that the staff had to have a plan to ensure everyone's safety—and to clean up the mess that would occur! Sure enough, they had a great time and the youth loved the activity. The next day the visits and calls to my office were numerous and intense. I redirected everyone to the youth staff by offering, "May I transfer you to the youth staff? They expressed their desire to hear and understand your concerns. It would be so much more valuable for the church and for them to hear directly from you!"

If attempts to coach have failed and you suspect rebellion, stubbornness, or arrogance as the causes of the disease, design a more direct approach. Before proceeding, ensure that all your documentation is in place and that you have clear, objective examples, records of your coaching attempts, and the support of your supervisors and other necessary people. Consider the use of an objective third party. When meeting with the offending staff member, explain the clear behavioral issues and give examples. Ask the person to put together an improvement plan that includes both a time schedule and accountability points to ensure that the plan is working. Don't allow the person to deflect the conversation by accusing you of not dealing with the problems correctly or by blaming others. Keep refocusing the staff member by saying that you'll address their concerns later, but right now you need them to address their plans to improve. Be ready for attempts to discredit you and the process you used, and for the person to employ others to help them fight this battle. Remember that obvious insubordination can't be tolerated. Take all acts of insubordination seriously, but don't overreact. Face them squarely and be prepared to offer or even require that the insubordinate person take some time off with pay to reflect on the consequences of their actions. Also communicate to the person that during their time away, the appropriate leaders on this staff will be examining the consequences of the insubordination and considering appropriate long-term action to deal with it. If the actions were so serious as to warrant it, implement a plan for dismissal.

When identifying the possible cause of this illness, don't confuse stubbornness with determination. Every effective and gifted leader that I've ever observed or worked with bordered on being stubborn. Their determination to do the right thing—to persevere in the midst of challenges and conflict for the sake of the institution where they served—was critical to their success. So how does one distinguish between the two? *Stubbornness* is based on a personal need to be right and to prove it to others. In contrast, *determination* is the conviction or deep understanding that one is doing what God wants. Determination conveys firmness and resolve. Stubbornness comes across as bullheaded, unyieldingly deciding to do something when the facts clearly suggest the wisdom of a different course of action. Yes, sometimes they are combined. Yet determination comes from taking a careful look at all the facts and the advice of others before deciding to act. Stubbornness tends to ignore all other factors and results in a decision not to yield—even in the face of reality.

When attempting to remedy insecurity resulting from an abnormal need for affirmation and recognition, try to provide wise, biblical, and pastoral advice, if requested. Otherwise, I use the same principles for dealing with deep-seated personal problems as described in other chapters of this book. Again, you need to decide whether to refer the staff member to a professional counselor or to a trusted pastoral counselor. I tend not to assume either of these roles with people I supervise or work with.

A Final Word

Staff high blood pressure, while serious and requiring treatment, usually does not indicate a fatal condition. However, the stubborn, arrogant, and rebellious forms of this illness can become fatal and do require swifter and more decisive treatments. At times this unfortunately includes removal from the body. The insecurity aspect of this infirmity calls for a rapid—but not rushed—remedy over a longer period of time. To be honest, I would choose to work with staff suffering from high blood pressure over those with low blood pressure—those needing help to push them into action. Directing a moving ship is always easier than getting a powerless ship underway.

7

Flaccidity of the Lips

Symptom: gossip is passed off as "prayer requests"

This illness includes the inability to maintain confidences and the improper use of prayer requests as veiled attempts to either discredit another person or spread the latest "juicy" news. While motives usually remain a mystery, many times this illness results from poor self-image, retaliation, or simply a need to make oneself feel more important by having the inside scoop. Unfortunately, this illness mostly reveals itself through secondhand sources and not from the person actually suffering from the illness. While mild forms of this illness exist in all of us, an extreme expression will destroy institutional communication and the ability to find trustworthy support when facing difficult struggles on a personal or professional level.

Major Signs of Illness

As the church secretary, Grace sat in the ultimate position of power. Nearly every bit of information—including minutes from committee meetings, confidences concerning members, and notes from the pastor to all staff members—crossed her desk at some point. The name of the church where she served was Grace Community, and though the church put out a weekly newsletter entitled "Grace Community Speaks," every insider understood that a far greater (and more deadly?) source of information existed. That fount of knowledge was called, tongue-in-cheek, "Grace Speaks." And it didn't refer to a printed paper that came in the mail.

When disaster struck a church member, inevitably the pastor was notified. He passed along the word to Grace, who would then (you could nearly time it: *three, two, one* . . .) pull out her church directory and call other church members . . . to solicit them to pray. Motivated out of pure concern, of course.

If one staff member received a dressing down (a common occurrence at Grace Community, unfortunately), Grace's fingers were busy dialing yet again. She gave no consideration to giving the briefest of details, either. Rather than a simple "our youth pastor has had a rough day and could use your prayers" (he generally was the one in trouble; dropping pumpkins off the roof at a youth rally wasn't his greatest show of discretion), a play-by-play of the original offense, the summons by the senior pastor, and the encounter were all fair game to be passed along. You might as well have put the poor guy on a rotisserie.

Charges were amplified, secrecy and confidences were disregarded, and any and all conversations among staff were "community property"—*Grace* community, as Grace the secretary defined it! Therefore, staff members resorted to nearly total silence in her presence (not much beyond "Good morning, Grace!" and "Good afternoon, Grace!" with a smile, of course). Committees led by staff often became clandestine; and at weekly staff devotional meetings, shared "prayer concerns" were given in a pretty vague and watered-down version for the sake of self-preservation. An environment of trust for ministering, working, and outreach as a team was nonexistent, except for those on the receiving end of Grace's calls.

The ultimate irony? The word *grace* means unmerited favor, receiving what you don't deserve. This Grace handed out what wasn't deserved, but she didn't do anyone any "favors," especially the wounded victims. Nor the church. Or the kingdom.

Cataloging the Signs of Illness

1. Improper disclosure of information when requesting prayer for others

Distinguishing between caring concern and improper disclosure can be difficult. You can identify the existence of this disease when the sharing starts to make you feel uncomfortable, when it subtly discredits or places the prayed-for person in a questionable light, or when the person sharing frequently knows too much about the personal situations of other people. Remember that those with a pastoral heart will generally seek out personal information in an effort to exercise loving concern. This is not a sign of the disease but rather just of a caring heart. With the new federal and state "right to privacy" laws, it is usually wise to instruct your staff to not share specifics when requesting prayer for another person. An exception would be if you have permission from the person to do so and also have asked for and received specific parameters concerning what he or she wants shared.

2. When confidential information you shared comes back to you through another person

When other staff members come to you asking for clarification about what you said to someone else—or asking something to the effect of "Did you really say that?"—then someone on staff is probably infected with flaccidity of the lips. Like with Typhoid Mary, sometimes locating the source of this disease can be difficult because people don't want to get another staff member in trouble or don't wish to be viewed as the office "snitch." It may be wise to ask some trusted staff about your hunches and concerns to see if they have some insight as to who might be at the center of spreading this illness.

3. When confidential information returns to you in a distorted form

This symptom means that you consistently discover that messages you gave to another person now return to you with key points or vital nuances missing, resulting in significant misunderstandings with potentially disastrous consequences. You could be discredited as a leader. You might also discover that information coming to you from a certain person is generally untrustworthy or that the person discloses too much inside information.

4. Receiving consistent feedback from numerous other staff members that "so-and-so can't be

trusted" or "you should be careful when talking to so-and-so"

Staff members have a way of alerting their leaders and other trusted staff of a problem—even when they don't want to directly identify the source of the problem. If you habitually receive indications that a staff person can't be trusted, you have probably located your source. Approach this information carefully until you have indisputable or multiple sources (preferably both) of proof that the suspected person is the leak. Remember that often the person who alerted you to the staff gossip will not want to be known as the one who blew the whistle on another staff member. In my experience, I have also been surprised by the way whistle-blowers can revise their original stories (given to you initially in private) by clouding the facts or lessening the intensity of their emotions or the certainty of their statements when later identified as the possible finger-pointer.

5. Discovering that vitally needed information is being withheld because people are fearful of how their information might be understood

When people are fearful of sharing information or of being misunderstood, you may need to face the reality of this illness in your midst. Getting full and correct information in order to make wise and informed decisions is always difficult. Skillfully working to ensure that you are correctly understood is always a valid concern also. However, when you find that too much information is being withheld or that people go to extreme means to ensure that they are being correctly understood, then this illness may be quietly destroying the trust level of your group. Remember that not all people like clear and direct communication styles, choosing instead to be more cautious and indirect. Try not to confuse differing communication styles with this symptom.

Treatment

The first step in silencing staff gossip requires a careful examination of yourself. Are *you* trustworthy and confidential? Have you inadvertently encouraged this illness through your actions or words? If so, depending on the level of your own involvement in this illness, a public statement seeking forgiveness and pledging repentance may be in order before proceeding. Ask trusted staff members who will lovingly and honestly tell you the truth if you are (1) guilty of this same illness or (2) subconsciously creating an environment that fosters the spread of this disease.

Build an open and trusting environment where information, analysis, and free-flowing ideas can emerge. Again, the leader normally sets the tone through modeling and taking the interpersonal risk of trusting others. Our goal at Denver Seminary is to ensure that our ministry team members hear from the senior administration team all the information they need to succeed in their roles as part of our team. This includes sharing the good, the bad, and the ugly in appropriate ways and settings. We ensure that we never share private or confidential information. If team members believe that private information will be inappropriately shared with others or that senior leaders do not trust them with needed information, then the communication wheel will grind to a screeching halt, endangering the institution.

If you have a solid relationship base with the suspected gossip, approach him or her as a caring friend and have an honest and gracious conversation. This may sound naive; however, sometimes people willingly accept feedback and correction if they trust the one doing the confronting. Try not to intensify the situation, and approach it in an evenhanded and kind fashion, explaining that you value him or her as a staff member. Explain that his or her contributions to your organization and respect as a staff member will only grow if he or she can bring this character flaw under control.

Once identified, that person needs to be confronted as soon as you can adequately prepare to do so. Locating the source of this illness will be difficult, but you should give the suspected person the benefit of the doubt unless you have indisputable proof. Even then, I try to believe that the person's motives are not malicious and instead result from character flaws that can be brought under the leadership of the Holy Spirit.

If you suspect a person but aren't sure or don't have good documentation, try a more indirect but clear approach: meet one-on-one with this person, expressing your concern that someone on staff may be violating confidences by sharing private information with others. Then explain how dangerous this distrustful behavior can be to staff morale and to the institution. Follow this statement with a question asking for his or her feedback on the importance of confidentiality and if he or she knows who might be spreading information. Be prepared for a wide range of responses, including full confession, denial, blaming others, falsely accusing others, or attacking you for suspecting him or her. Listen carefully and respond accordingly to the response you receive. If the person questions your motives in asking, respond by saying how important it is that all staff members act in a trustworthy fashion and that you are soliciting his or her help in ensuring that this value is upheld. If the person asks if you are accusing him or her of being the "leak," respond by saying that (1) you desire that all staff members be trustworthy, (2) you are in the initial stages of an investigation to determine who might be at the source of the problem, and finally, (3) you hoped that he or she might be of help. This approach can prove risky, but it could also provide an indirect warning to the person that the behavior has to stop *now*. Use sparingly and only when it seems wise.

When certain of the source, proceed once you have documented objective *and* indisputable *evidence*. Ensure that the people giving you the evidence are committed to their stories and facts. I prefer multiple witnesses rather than only one source. Prayerfully consider involving a third party, and remember the principles of documentation as explained in previous chapters. When meeting with the offending party, describe the unacceptable behavior with the documented proof, and then listen carefully. If the offending party confesses, then respond in a pastoral fashion—granting forgiveness, affirming the person, and defining appropriate repentance through the agreed-upon next steps. Remember to keep the offending party fully responsible for these future action steps. I rarely assume an ongoing role in the corrective process other than in my role of holding that person accountable for the changes. Finding another trusted friend to more closely work with the offending party has proven extremely wise, in my experience.

If the offending party denies the truth or blames others, restate the proof. Usually this response is followed by the standard charge that the biblical principles for confronting another have not been followed. Mostly this is a defense mechanism attempting to (1) deflect the blame to others or (2) catch you off guard so that you will use your energies to defend yourself or the integrity of the process instead of confronting the offender with the truth. *Don't fall into this trap.* Instead, restate the evidence and ask the offending party to answer the evidence that is being presented. At times I will simply respond with, "Those are issues for another time. Right now we need to focus our attention on the fact that you have acted in an untrustworthy manner and on how you are going to assume full responsibility for changing your behavior." Many times at this juncture the conversations escalate into tears, incredulousness, and personal attacks upon the person (or people) doing the confronting. When reaching an impasse like this, you can end the meeting with the statement that we are no longer making significant progress and that you are going to give the offending party a chance to meet again after he or she has had time to carefully reflect upon these matters. This approach has worked for me in the past, but at times it meant that the offending party marshaled his or her forces and rebuttals and returned ready for war the next time we met! Again, this demonstrates the importance of wisdom within the moment and context.

Another option (based upon the indisputable nature of the facts) is to proceed with an agreed-upon range of actions such as dismissal, suspension, probation, or demotion. The severity of the offense helps to determine which course of action might be wisest. When implementing these options, be prepared to take criticism from others who choose to defend the suspected person or from people who agree with the decision but are uncertain about the facts of what really happened. Remember to keep the details confidential, and resist the temptation to exonerate yourself in the public arena.

A Final Word

Some might suggest that you should just wait and allow God to take care of all staff problems, especially when dealing with unpaid staff. Waiting upon God and prayerfully asking God to deal with an unpaid or paid staff problem is one of the few universal principles that should always be applied to every staff challenge. Be careful not to confuse insecurity or conflict avoidance with waiting upon God. On the other hand, don't proceed too quickly without allowing for prayerful reflection and listening to God for wisdom on how to proceed. In my experience, 95 percent of the time (what do they say about statistics being made up on the spot?), after I gave the matter time and careful prayer, God still chose to involve me directly in the solution to the problem. Unfortunately, I can't let you off the hook for confrontation by admitting that this was due to my lack of faith or a powerless prayer life. On the contrary, it's just generally the way God prefers to see things done. For effective leadership, the sticky wicket of confrontation is a constant reality!

8

Lack of Large
Motor Coordination

Symptom: a habitual pattern of arriving late

In addition to the tendency to be late, people with this illness have a propensity to firmly believe that their lives and daily responsibilities are more difficult to manage than most everyone else's. Therefore, they believe that others should accommodate their tardiness. This disease is also usually accompanied by a chronic inability to complete assignments on time. Left undiagnosed and unattended, the disease is potentially infectious, quickly spreading like a plague throughout the entire staff—volunteer and paid.

Major Signs of Illness

Carolyn describes this illness with the following story from her experience.

We had hurried the kids through homework assignments, wolfed down our dinner in record time, and broken every speed limit to get to church—all so that we would be on time for a planning meeting. Even though Craig was not leading the committee, please understand that "on time" meant at least twenty minutes early. We made it, but we brought along upset stomachs (a likely consequence when you eat tacos in ten minutes), exasperation (I had forgotten the notes I'd jotted that afternoon), and bad attitudes (all that panic for nothing, considering that we were *thirty* minutes early). I'd be playacting the happy little wife that evening when I was actually steaming!

Committee members arrived over the next half hour, but the member we most needed that evening—as he was the chair—sauntered in a full fifteen minutes past the hour. That was frustrating enough, considering our considerable efforts to arrive when we did. (I assumed the others had been through similar experiences to arrive on time, considering that we all looked a bit harried and frayed around the edges.) But it was his cavalier response that rankled the most: "Late? Oh, for me being on time is at least ten minutes late. You'll get used to it!"

Grrrrrrr. . . .

With careful advance planning, I was determined not to repeat the mad dash for our next meeting. I prepared dinner ahead so that it only needed to be put on the table, clothes were chosen and laid out, and I'd placed my notes right next to my purse. Nothing but calm preparation and an organized exit this time out of the stall! But who would've foreseen that one of our kids would need a several-step science project completed that night? Or that an entire bottle of pop would end up on the floor? We experienced yet another frantic drive to church, only to arrive again in plenty of time.

And the other committee members? Having gleaned that the chair could (and would) arrive late, most surmised that this had become "standard operating procedure." Granted, there were a couple time-conscious people (like my husband) who arrived dutifully, found seats around the table, and were prepared to begin right on time. But most trickled in over the next half hour, arriving ten to fifteen minutes late. And the chair? He graced us with his presence at a full twenty minutes past the designated start time.

The disease had become highly infectious, and an immediate cure was desperately needed. Otherwise, those who appreciated arriving on time would be too frustrated to stay on the committee, and our effectiveness and ability to get anything accomplished was seriously threatened. And Craig was already one step from strangling this staff member.

Well, not really. I am exaggerating, as Craig would've been much more humane and empathetic. He was merely considering several forms of medieval torture.

Cataloging the Signs of Illness

1. *Repeated tardiness to meetings or other scheduled events, accompanied by last-minute, dramatic entrances*

My personal favorite is the "traffic was terrible" excuse, especially when other members of the team had the same commute and navigated it through advanced planning. Even more annoying is when these folks use the traffic excuse a second and third time for a regularly scheduled event. Addressing the issue the first time it occurs with a soft statement like, "Please ensure that you make the necessary adjustments to be on time for our next meeting" can prohibit future instances and send a signal of your expectations.

2. Habitual inability to complete assignments on time, or presenting unfinished projects on the due date

We all know that sometimes unforeseeable or uncontrollable factors can prevent us from completing a project on time. However, frequent and persistent patterns of late assignments substantiate this diagnosis. Usually this symptom indicates that work on the project was either started too late or improperly managed throughout the process. Generally, when an assignment deadline is missed, you should request that all completed work to that point be given to you for review. This enables you to diagnose how severe the illness may be.

3. Convoluted excuses that grow in intensity and complexity

When you discover in attempting to clarify the details of the excuses that they've become elaborate to the point of being unbelievable, you are usually facing an extreme case. And if you regularly find yourself scratching or shaking your head—or you reach the level of being fatigued from trying to make sense of a staff member's excuses—it is time to face the reality of this illness.

4. Repeated irresponsibility accompanied by an inviting, engaging personality or an unusually strong public talent (e.g., vocal performance)

These signs may indicate that a staff member has probably been suffering from this disease throughout his or her lifetime. Most likely he or she learned early in life that using one's personality strength or an outstanding talent in a certain fashion can eliminate the hard work that comes with developing the discipline and skills of managing life. This staff member probably grew up in an environment where allowances were granted *because of* this engaging personality or unusual talent. My point? It takes a lifetime to make an irresponsible person and therefore much hard, persistent work to help this person overcome the tendency to rest on their personality or talent. Treatment will be complicated. Remember to always keep the person in charge of their professional and personal improvements.

5. Dependence on the public affirmation that comes from being extremely talented or having an engaging personality

Over a lifetime, this person has probably neglected the hard work of a disciplined life in areas where affirmation is rare and instead given all his or her energies to those things that provide the most recognition. Treating this symptom requires a different approach than for the previous one. "Overly dependent on public affirmation" refers to staff members who have spent their lifetime living according to the thoughts and judgments of others. They are fearful to face their true self or true desires. Hiding behind a manufactured image that has successfully produced public affirmation, they will not risk the possible rejection of trying to develop new skills or talents. Often this symptom is combined with the one described in point 4, but this is not always true.

6. Responding to confrontation with robust defensiveness, a refusal to stay on topic, an

attempt to make the confronter defensive, or blaming others

It's very unlikely that you'll receive the humble response of "Thank you for bringing this to my attention" and "I will work hard to improve in these areas because I desire to honor God with all aspects of my life." Instead, the most common responses are defensiveness or attempts to deflect the conversation by pointing out that this confrontation did not correctly follow the biblical pattern. If you are not persistent in keeping the focus on the need for the person to improve, you will find yourself spending your energy on trying to convince this person that the process was indeed correct. Try hard not to allow this deflection attempt to take you off track. When a staff member attempts to distract our conversation from the main point, I normally respond by saying, "I hear your concern, and we can discuss that at another time. Right now the issue of your being irresponsible is the main focus of our conversation. So please help me to brainstorm some ways you can improve in this area." Remember that a response that is defensive or deflects blame to others is a reliable indicator that the person suffers from this illness.

Treatment

Confront the person who exhibits signs of chronic lateness. Left unchecked, this illness becomes an infection that can rapidly spread throughout an entire staff. This frequently occurs because others grow discouraged with the hard work and discipline they invest in your organization in order to do things well. Whether paid or unpaid, staff members exhibiting signs of this illness need urgent and careful treatment.

Start all your meetings promptly when scheduled *and make it clear to all those arriving late that you expect them to be on time.* I usually begin all the meetings I am leading with prayer. Having late arrivers enter during a time of prayer can send a message that encourages them to be on time for the next meeting. When diagnosing repeated failure to make a meeting on time, go privately to that person and state your expectation that they be punctual. If the pattern continues, go to them again and explain the accountability that will be implemented if they continue to arrive late. I have also used gimmicks to signal to everyone the need to be on time. Some of these are: publicly thanking those who were on time; commenting that we show respect to all members of the team when we arrive promptly; establishing a late jar so that when people arrive late, they are required to put a dollar in the jar, and when the money reaches a sufficient amount, we use it to provide snacks for the next meeting.

Before attempting to coach or intervene, prepare all the necessary documentation, listing the clearly identifiable and persistent behavior issues. You must also provide objective examples that can be confirmed by multiple sources. The key is to first build your case on paper before sharing it with the person suffering from this illness.

Give the staff member the benefit of the doubt, choosing to believe that no previous leaders have taken the time to teach him or her how to be responsible. Ron was an extremely talented and well-liked staff member at one of the churches where I served. But he was frustrating everyone with his tardiness, inability to get things done, and mad rush, "crisis at the last minute" style. In his case, I discovered that no one in his life had invested the time to simply teach him how to plan ahead and organize. Ron had learned to make excuses or use his talent (which was usually strong enough to allow him to slide by without advance planning) to divert people from seeing his inabilities in this area. So I approached him and asked if he would be willing to meet with me for a period of time to learn how to organize his work for even more effective ministry results. To my amazement, he readily agreed. Over the next six weeks, we worked together to develop a system for planning ahead and organizing his work and his team's work to ensure that projects were effectively completed on time. Ron will never have a natural ability to plan and organize, but he learned how to make peace with this aspect of ministry and allow others to assist him. The last time I heard from Ron, he shared how advance planning and organization has enhanced the effectiveness of both his personality and his outstanding talent.

Some who suffer from this illness may think it's impossible to change. Try to help them see that a minimal amount of planning can bring rewarding results. Lastly, show them how to use computer software and tools that exist to help in this area; these can help them break needed improvements into more manageable steps.

Find a mentor for this person. Sometimes I discover that people suffering with this illness are afraid that advance planning or organization will diminish their personality strength or outstanding talent. Since I am a natural organizer, this seems nonsensical to me, but it is a very real concern to them. My trying to convince them otherwise has never worked. One approach I have used is to recruit another staff member with talent or a strong personality who has previously worked through this issue. That person can tell the story of how advance planning and organization actually enhanced their ministry effectiveness. This mentoring can eliminate some resistance and open the person to an ongoing relationship to help them improve.

Suggest professional counseling. When this illness is deeply embedded into the psyche of the person, professional counseling may be required. Carefully approach this aspect of the illness. My real-life experience and other experts suggest that you as the supervisor should generally refrain from assuming any counseling role. Even if you are professionally trained, it may prove wise to not blur your professional relationship with the staff member by assuming a counseling role with him or her. In these tenuous situations, holding the staff member responsible for making clearly defined behavior changes in a specific time framework may work best. Gentle and persuasive encouragement to seek professional counseling may also be included. In the midst of these conversations, I tend to say something like, "To assist you in making these changes, you may find that seeking professional counsel into why you seem to consistently miss deadlines and assignments will help. If you would like, I can recommend a couple of resources you might contact." In some situations I have stated, "Your continuation on this staff requires you to make these needed changes, and I suggest that you seek professional counseling to ensure your success." This second line is much harsher and effective only in situations where previous attempts to solve these issues have failed and more gentle persuasion to seek counseling has been disregarded. Since I have personally benefited from professional counseling, I sometimes also briefly explain how seeking counsel in my life was difficult to initiate but very helpful. This amount of sharing must be appropriate to the actual situation you face and to the strength of your relationship with this staff person. Obviously, it also needs to be true.

Legal experts seem to be divided on whether an organization can require that an employee seek professional counseling when dealing with such an issue. You may want to seek the counsel of your institutional attorneys before proceeding on this track.

When implementing treatment, ensure that you have full support from all necessary supervisors and any significant informal leaders such as elders, deacons, and donors, who might be recruited to join this staff member for a confrontation. Those suffering from this illness will test whether you are acting alone and whether you have the appropriate support and authority for the changes you are requiring. Careful documentation of the lack of performance and the required behavioral changes and accountability needs to be in place before approaching these staff members. Allowing the necessary supervisors to give input and sign off on the documentation may also prove extremely beneficial. When approaching informal lay leaders of the church, it may be appropriate to ensure privacy and limit your discussion to poor behaviors that can be sustained by numerous witnesses. Explain to the lay leader the process you are following and your desire to help this staff member improve for the benefit of the organization and for him- or herself. If your organization has a personnel committee, enlist their full support and assistance. If the staff member has resisted coaching attempts on how to become more organized, never proceed with treating this illness until you are carefully prepared for a full skirmish.

Hire an assistant to take responsibility for organizing the ministry for an ill staff member if the staff member is indispensable to the organization and is willing to improve. Carefully consider this option. Sometimes the staff member will resent this new person and judge that you are imposing too much control over his or her area. Or the person recruited to assist the suffering staff member may be placed in a difficult place with too much conflict and passive-aggressive behavior on the part of the ill staff member. At other times, this option may be unwise if it encourages the staff member to become even more irresponsible or sends a signal to other members of the staff that being irresponsible could result in their getting more staff. Christian organizations that use this approach to compensate for a large number of staff members who suffer from this disease spread the resources of their organization too thin. They eventually weaken their ability to successfully complete their mission. Needing two people to do one person's job usually represents poor stewardship and leadership. Sometimes wisely and gracefully releasing the staff person is the best option for the organization.

A Final Word

Frankly, I've found this illness to be the least responsive to treatment. Those suffering have a propensity to fight back, recruit others to join the fight, deny reality, and run from attempts to cure. They will go to extreme measures to keep from facing the reality of their illness and assuming responsibility for treatment. This is probably the one area where I have personally seen the least amount of positive, long-lasting results. When persistently required to make the necessary deep-scated changes to improve, staff members usually resign or go elsewhere. In spite of these negative tendencies, leaving this infection unchecked will only spread the disease throughout your staff. Others will start to believe that meeting high ministry expectations is not necessary in your organization. And that belief is a malignancy that a leader dare not allow.

9

Permanent Paralysis

Symptom: an urgent ministry need merely leads to . . .
        inertia

The illness develops quickly in this manner: "We have an immediate and serious problem, so let's form a sub-committee and ask the members to research the issues and then report to our full committee for their consideration so they can pass it on to the elders for their decision on how we can develop a ministry to help!"

Sound familiar? The result should also. In another six months such a ministry *might* be ready to address this "urgent" need.

Major Signs of Illness

Even though no one would admit it, the organizational structure at the church where I served early in my ministry experience was designed to control, hinder change, and ensure that no new programs were established at the church. An odd way to define "stability" or "careful process," wasn't it? In all the organizational structures where I have served, this one frustrated me most.

Here's how it worked. If individual staff members or teams identified a need or wanted to implement a new program, they had to gain approval on at least four levels. The steps consisted of jumping through the hoops of (1) the full staff, (2) the appropriate subcommittee, (3) the full committee, and lastly (4) the entire deacon board for final approval. One year we even expanded the structure (claiming it was an "improved process") by establishing a new church board that would review the work of the deacons.

Other key components were that the committees met monthly and no new business could be put on a committee's agenda without two weeks' notice. Equally disturbing was the fact that all the subcommittees, the full committees, the deacons, and the church board had to meet the *same week of the month*.

So let's do the math.

First, the full staff approved an idea or proposal; they met twice a month. Then, if the staff approved in time to get their recommendation on the subcommittee's agenda, the subcommittee would review their recommendation. If it was approved by the subcommittee, the full committee would consider their recommendation. Then, if approved and time allowed, the full committee would pass it on to the deacons. Usually this happened a month later in order to meet the two-week requirement. Finally, the deacons would consider the recommendation, and if they approved, it was passed on to the new church board. Confused yet?

If my math is correct, that totals eighteen weeks or four and one-half months. That was *if* all went well.

The following scenario, however, was more likely to happen: somewhere along the way a committee would table the issue because they needed more information, thus delaying the entire process by another month. This sent the entire process back to square one to start up again. It's a wonder that the original need and recommendation were even remembered by the end of that journey!

In the four years I served there, I do not believe more than six significant decisions were made. But oh, how we prided ourselves on our biblical, thorough process! Is it any wonder that the church closed its doors about ten years ago? Quite frankly, I'm surprised there were enough people at the end to fill the required committee slots to make the decision to close!

Cataloging the Signs of Illness

1. Confusing control with mobilizing ministry

At some point in time, many church leaders made the decision that people and teams could not be trusted and required redundant supervision. Or perhaps we started to believe that multiple levels of oversight would ensure that we stayed faithful to our original beliefs and purposes. However, let me emphatically state this: appropriate trust and empowerment are the counterbalance to over-controlling. Committees exist in an organization to mobilize people and resources into ministry—not to control them. Certainly appropriate oversight and controls are mandatory. Too many unaccountable leaders have damaged the reputation of Christ and the church. This illness, however, is about too much focus on control and not enough on freeing people to *do* ministry. The church's mission is to get people out of meetings—where they only talk about ministering—and involved in the lives of those desperately needing the gospel and Christian care.

2. Confusing talking about ministry with doing ministry

Too many organizations are structured in this manner because the leaders confuse talking about ministry (i.e., committee work) with doing ministry. Far too many resources and too much time are spent analyzing ideas instead of implementing ministry. Yes, we must pray and strategically reflect before acting. However, this illness is about taking our best leaders away from significant involvement in the lives of those in need and placing them on redundant committees doing meaningless tasks. Unfortunately, we Christians have a tendency to retreat from engaging the people of the world for Christ. Committees might be disguising a "holy appearing huddle" that only draws us away from significant ministry.

3. Existing committees have no authority

If groups of people within an organization are regularly convened to address issues or make recommendations and are not given any authority or responsibility to implement changes, the organization suffers from this disease. Most gifted staff members will not serve on committees where their work means nothing more than making recommendations to another team who will do the same work and then decide for themselves. Recently I received a letter asking for volunteers to serve on our community's regional planning commission. I was somewhat interested in serving in this capacity until I saw the footnote that stated, "This planning commission serves solely as a recommendation committee for the county commission." In other words, "Please do all the work and pass on your recommendations, and then we will review them briefly and then decide what should be done!" Guess what? I did not apply.

4. Taking too much time or involving too many groups to make decisions

How frustrating to have a passion and vision for a particular need within the community and know that it will take months and enormous effort to help your church see the need and deal with its bureaucratic systems! No wonder so many gifted Christian leaders are establishing ministries outside of the church on such a frequent basis. Responses to disasters are notable examples. Many local churches are still trying to figure out how they can best respond to the disasters that occurred throughout the world in the last year. Meanwhile, other organizations have been sending people and resources for months, already making a significant difference in the name of Christ.

5. Declining morale, volunteerism, resources, and overall numbers

These can be regular indicators of permanent paralysis. People will not stay in or support organizations that focus on control and hindering change. They desire to support and participate in meaningful ministries where they feel supported and encouraged—and especially desire to see the results in the lives of others. Look around and count the number of gifted leaders within your organization. If that total is lower than you thought or desire, you may be suffering from this disease.

6. Too much authority located in one area

Gifted staff members will not serve long within organizations that give too much control to one leader or team within the organization. These leaders are not rejecting biblical leadership and authority. Rather, they are asking their leaders and organizations to serve and operate in the biblical fashion of equipping the team members (the saints) for the work of the ministry. They desire organizational leaders who empower and assist them in finding and fulfilling God's call in their lives, and they are not interested in watching others do ministry or spending hours working to ensure that everything is right before ministry efforts are sanctioned or launched. We should be about competently training people and mobilizing effective ministry with responsive leaders and organizational systems.

Treatment

Frankly, this illness resists treatment and tends to be systemic. Leaders within these organizations have control and usually are reluctant to relinquish their positions of power. Many of these leaders have well-meaning motives but are uncomfortable with—or are not trained to lead—the massive changes necessary to restructure their organizations with a focus on mobilizing ministry. So many of these types of organizations are in a "death rattle" and need help to make massive turnarounds. They also may need to simply close their doors. I find that young, emerging leaders tend to avoid these organizations, and nothing can be more fatal than a lack of emerging leaders to provide renewed energy and passion.

A more positive approach is to replace your committees with ministry teams. In contrast to most committees, those who will constitute your ministry teams are those actually *doing the ministry*. Explain the parameters of their authority and your reporting expectations. Discuss items like budget constraints, spending, and reporting policies; how to request more resources; when to report problems or possible conflict; and when a decision should be referred to the next level of authority. Flattening and streamlining your authority structure is crucial. Ensure that the ministry teams have the authority, resources, and communication mechanisms to successfully complete their mission. Coaching them to write a specific mission statement or purpose for their ministry team can also help to sharpen their focus and work.

Remember that people and organizations respond better to multiplication than subtraction. One way to eventually replace your committees is by working with the committee leadership to develop and empower ministry teams within their spheres of influence. Recruit committee chairs and church leaders who understand and support this change and ask them to implement this change within their areas. Once the momentum of excitement builds about the new ministry teams, ask the church leaders to consider reorganizing the entire structure to reflect this type of approach. Using short-term task forces that have a limited range of responsibility and a specific time frame in which to complete their work may help. Discipline yourself to disband these task forces and not perpetuate their existence once they complete their task. With this approach you are attempting to build organization-wide momentum and excitement that will provide the base for you to replace your current committee structure with ministry teams. If the ministry team members can share their excitement concerning the new approach, soon even some of the most committed to committee structure may be gently persuaded to make the change. Tell the stories of these successful ministry teams in as many places and ways as you can.

Ask the elders or deacons to hire an outside consultant to analyze your organization and make recommendations on how your organization could be better organized to accomplish your mission. Be careful not to become overly dependent upon this consultant. Hire someone who will teach and coach you and your team in identifying and making the changes. The vital components are strengthening your institution's leadership and implementing the structure that will enable your institution to reach its God-given dreams and mobilize your members into important ministry for the spread of the gospel.

Another workable solution would be to find ways to wisely and efficiently work within your organization's existing structures. This approach builds trust and provides the depth of relationships needed for future change. You can't do a lot in one year, but you can do much more than you would think possible in three to five years. Take a more long-range approach, praying and asking God to create the motivation for change within your organization; also ask him to send leaders who will assist you in this change. God honors this prayer and approach. Do not use a long-range approach if you are in the midst of a major turnaround situation where the future existence of the institution is at stake.

Prayerfully listen, reflect, journal, and ask God and trusted leaders within your organization to reveal which of these approaches might work best for your specific situation.

A Final Word

Overcoming permanent paralysis takes rigorous rehabilitation and an ability to cope with the pain of resistance. Recently I fell off a ladder, landing flat on my back on the cement floor of my basement. Fortunately, I only suffered a slight fracture in my right elbow. However, overcoming the pain and maintaining the hard work to restore flexibility in my lower back and hips has taken months of exercise combined with anti-inflammatory drugs. Nothing I could do would shorten my recovery time; trying to proceed too fast only introduces unnecessary pain. Please understand that treating this illness usually means a systemic effort requiring intense prayer. Then it will take months or even years to see real change. Match the speed of your change initiative to the health of your institution.

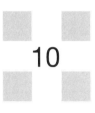

10

Narcissism

Symptom: what do you do when you are the problem?

You're probably thinking, narcissism is a psychological disorder, not a physical ailment. True, but self-love and too much attention to one's sense of importance are too prevalent in Christian leadership to ignore in a book on leading staff. Therefore, this chapter intends to honestly address this subtle and yet most dangerous illness.

Major Signs of Illness

So why is it always about you? A book I read on marriage a few years ago addressed the issue of giving more attention to the needs of one spouse at the expense of the other. I thought it would be good for Carolyn and me to discuss this chapter together—basically because I judged we were doing so well in balancing this tension. (Do I dare admit that I was waiting for praise from Carolyn on how good I was in this area?) So when I gave her a copy of the chapter, I prefaced it by saying, "This is an area where we do well, but I thought it would be interesting to at least discuss it." To my utter amazement, she responded by saying, "Actually, I don't think we do well in this area at all. It *is* generally always about you and your work."

Ouch! That frank assessment wounded and bewildered me, especially in light of the fact that she was one hundred percent correct. It took a lot of pretty intense conversations, soul searching, and adjustments in life on my part to sort through this discrepancy. I had been hiding behind the idea that I was doing God's work and therefore that justified my self-absorption.

Wondering how this story applies to serving on a staff? It definitely relates to the fact that in all healthy human relationships and social structures, attention and power need to be appropriately balanced. As leaders, we need to create ways for all members of the staff to contribute, feel appreciated, share in the power of the organization, and know they have a part in shaping the present and future of the organization. Yet for a variety of reasons, senior leaders can easily fall into the trap of allowing too much focus and power to fall on them.

I have heard—and unfortunately personally used—numerous justifications for this tendency. As many have said, far too much praise goes to the senior leader when things are going well—and likewise, far too much blame when things are going poorly. Still, senior leaders are critical to the health and success of any organization. We just go too far at times with that simplistic analogy.

A friend recently conveyed the following story that illustrates this issue. When she was visiting a new church, the service started with a trumpet fanfare, all the congregation standing, and the senior pastor (accompanied solely by his spouse) promenading down the aisle of the church to the platform. Once the pastor and his wife were seated, the congregation sat down and applauded their entrance. No, unfortunately I have *not* fabricated this story as an illustration! Isn't this a deplorable example of self-importance and absorption with one's own power? Needless to say, my friend did not make a second visit to that church!

In staff situations, this malady can reveal itself by senior leaders' desires to keep all power in their hands; therefore, they tend to be controlling, apply centralized decision making, use poor delegation, and generally feel threatened by talented staff. Sometimes this happens because senior leaders think they possess the most wisdom—or that God speaks only through them. In a subtle progression, these leaders get used to being listened to and deferred to because of their positions of power. Sometimes this occurs because they possess some exceptional gifts like preaching or leading. Regardless, this tendency to control through one's office—for whatever reason—is wrong. The unfortunate result is that the growth of the entire organization is stunted. This chapter will attempt to examine the nuances of this malady and offer treatment—remedies which, I must admit, are extremely difficult to implement.

Cataloging the Signs of Illness

1. When all decision making centers in your office

At one church I know of, long lines of staff members form outside the executive pastor's office on a regular basis. The staff members know that their prescribed roles are to carry out the wishes of the senior and executive pastor—never implementing any changes without first securing the executive pastor's approval. In essence, the staff members are laborers for the two senior leaders and have almost no power and freedom to think. When confronted with their behavior, the two leaders responded by saying that things go easier when they know everything that is happening and can prevent staff members from making unnecessary mistakes.

Ask yourself these questions: Do you give too many answers when asked a ministry question? Or do you instead encourage other staff members to think for themselves and then make their own decisions? When staff members bring problems, do you request that they first analyze the situation and, even more importantly, also bring possible solutions for you to interact with? Do you feel threatened or defensive when others challenge your thinking? Are you convinced that you really *do* know more or are wiser than the majority of your staff? And lastly, do your staff members demonstrate an inability to make decisions and take risks?

2. Impatience or a lack of ability to listen to others

Frankly, I have worked hard over the last thirty years to become a good listener. While people tell me that I do this well, listening is not a natural gift for me, and I must work hard to demonstrate that I am indeed listening and valuing the person who is talking. I can easily start to form my opinions or reactions well before those talking have finished processing their thoughts with me. At times this appears to be impatience on my part; at other times it simply looks like I'm not listening. My true desire is to listen well and seek understanding, but I must work hard to be a good listener.

Some of my gifts have been helpful in ministry leadership, but they also can be easily misunderstood. For example, I have always been able to process large amounts of information at an accelerated pace and often well ahead of others. Because of this, sometimes people think that I make snap decisions or come to strong conclusions too quickly. Yes, this can be true; however, I have found that many times I have indeed processed the factors surrounding the issue just as thoroughly as others—only much quicker. Regardless, the issue is that *good listening ensures that the person speaking feels heard and understood.* Sometimes those struggling with listening are external processors who need to talk in order to form and understand their opinions. When they take long periods to process out loud, they appear to be poor listeners, and this can indeed be the case.

Another area that I must consciously control is my ability to debate. Many (including Carolyn!) tell me that I can come across as intimidating because of the analytical strength of my thinking and arguing. Extreme forms of this illness can be expressed as an arrogant belief that the leader is the only truly gifted thinker in the group and that others' opinions need to be tolerated but are of little importance. When staff members believe the only profitable way to share an opinion with you is to make it appear as though *you* thought of it—then you know you are in trouble.

3. Delegating without giving proper authority or with too many limits

How frustrating for others when they are given large levels of responsibility—but are not empowered with sufficient authority to complete their tasks! At one of the churches where I served, the staff were limited in their use of church credit cards to a total of $500. Yet when some of the youth staff led a mission trip overseas with fifty senior high students in tow, they knew that the credit card spending limit would not be sufficient if an emergency occurred. They also did not want to carry large amounts of cash.

When I suggested to the CFO that we allow the youth staff a limit of $2,500, World War III broke out. He was thoroughly convinced that this increased limit would restrict his ability to control the expenses of the church and the staff. On another occasion he tried to limit the number of pizzas that could be purchased by staff for any ministry occasions and, with humorous results, to control which pizza parlor could be used without his prior approval! Think of the logic in this way: we had entrusted the very lives of all those youth into our youth pastors' care, but we could *not* trust the staff to spend $2,500, to make wise decisions in emergency situations, or even to order the correct amount of pizza. It was all about this CFO's desire to control.

Another form of this ailment is the inability to delegate without taking back the responsibility or dramatically altering the decisions of those to whom the responsibility was delegated. How frustrating to be told that you had the responsibility to lead and then later discover that your real job was to guess what the leader wanted and complete the task that way. The senior pastor at one church I observed had given a committee the task of selecting paint colors for remodeling the children's area. When the committee shared their decisions, the senior pastor, to our great surprise, rejected their choices and selected a palette of colors that were just plain ugly. When the time came for people to volunteer to paint the rooms, the senior pastor was shocked that so few people showed up to help paint with his ugly color choices! If you struggle with delegation, you may suffer from this ailment.

4. Thinking you are entitled to preferential treatment because of your role

This one is tough to identify *and* accept. Attitudes of denial and entitlement are difficult to resist and overcome. Like a blizzard in the mountains, they can start slowly and then become blinding whiteouts, blocking your ability to see.

Denver Seminary moved to a new campus in the summer of 2005. When assigning designated parking spaces, we chose to only reserve spots for disability needs, our guests, our chancellor (who is ninety-three), and our apartment residents. All the rest of us—including me, the president—would fend for ourselves in the midst of the numerous demands for parking. I wish I could say that all of the senior leaders, faculty, and staff here at the seminary accepted this decision with grace and dignity. I *wish* I could, but I know how much I don't like walking long distances to the office—especially on cold and snowy days. Don't people understand how busy my schedule is?

5. *Feeling threatened or intimidated by other talented staff*

A friend who serves as an elder in his church disclosed that the senior pastor had just requested (in reality, demanded) that the elders fire two staff members because they were not respecting his authority as leader. The elders carefully asked key questions to diagnose the real issues. To their amazement, they could not find any legitimate justification for the senior pastor's criticism of the two staff members, and they also knew that the congregation loved these two people. When asked, the senior pastor could not offer any objective examples to prove her allegations. What was the real problem? These two staff members were too well liked and respected on staff, and the senior pastor felt threatened by their expertise.

Now, it's easy to read that story and think of others who suffer from the same disease. The tougher task is to read that story and think of the times when *you and I* have felt intimidated by talented people. Maybe we didn't begin a vendetta to have them fired or demoted, but did we subconsciously diminish their giftedness by listening less? Or by not asking for their opinions when we knew they would be valuable? Or did we pass them over for a responsibility that they were equal to? These subtle effects of our intimidation by talented people are just as dangerous because ultimately, we hinder the development of ministry—and people.

6. Needing to be the best and brightest in the room

Some leaders diminish the strength and growth of their organizations because they have to be recognized as the best and brightest in the room. If this is true, no one who is more talented or gifted than this leader can find the space to lead alongside him or her. My motto? *Don't try to be the best and brightest in the room. Instead, try to get the best and brightest in the room with you.* In the end you will look much wiser, and your organization will reach even higher levels of mission fulfillment. Even if that does sound a bit narcissistic, ultimately, I still believe that actively recruiting people who are smarter and better than you is the correct approach.

Treatment

Embrace the reality of this infirmity. This may be the toughest stage before healing can begin. None of us is immune to this sickness/sin. These tendencies lurk behind the activities of each day, waiting for the opportunity to seize the moment to take over and define our leadership styles. Recognizing these tendencies and then building a lifestyle of consistent honesty and openness to feedback from God and others are the foundational steps.

Practice preventive approaches. It is not a matter of our trying harder or becoming more committed. Rather, it is about a consistent, ongoing regimen: we must be regularly living in the presence of Christ and the power of the Holy Spirit by applying the spiritual disciplines. People relate best to different spiritual disciplines. Some prefer fasting or serving the poor as the primary ways to apply spiritual disciplines to their daily lives. I connect more deeply to the practices of Scripture reading, prayer, journaling, retreat, silence, and listening as counterbalances to my tendency to too greatly define my relationship with Christ through my actions. I must admit that I more regularly sense God's presence and power in the actual role of serving. However, by creating quiet spaces through these other spiritual disciplines, I now tend to serve more out of Christ's love for me than out of a desire to prove my prowess as a leader. Please do not misunderstand that statement—I have not totally eliminated these tendencies of narcissism. Practicing spiritual disciplines provides needed environments where the Spirit of God can transform me and build into my life the power needed to control this disease.

Define acceptable parameters for decision making and authority. Using a group discussion method, work together to explain when a staff member can make decisions without first seeking approval. Consider some of these following parameters: when a decision is consistent with the institution's mission, vision, values, and budget/spending limits, the staff member has the authority to decide without seeking a supervisor's approval. Safety and respect for others must always be upheld. We also use the "front page of the local paper" test here at the seminary. That means asking, "If what I am about to do were to show up on the front page of the local newspaper, could it withstand public scrutiny?" Even more important is the question, "Will what I am about to do bring honor or dishonor to the name of Christ and the reputation of this organization?" Remind the staff members that once parameters for authority are established, they will still be accountable for all decisions made. One final principle to consider when establishing decision-making parameters for staff: recommend that if in doubt, they talk it out with their supervisor.

Ask staff members to bring possible solutions—not just problems—when seeking your help in making a decision. Ask what they are thinking and whether they have come to any conclusions; this reinforces your commitment to creating a thinking staff. Probing how and why they are thinking about something or how they came to a conclusion about a problem can also teach the staff members how to think for themselves. Then, when appropriate, offer some additional ideas for them to consider and end the conversation by saying, "I trust you and will support whatever decision you think is best." And what if their ideas are crazy? Speak the truth in love and offer other options for them to consider while you attempt to help them make wise decisions. Try not to ever make a decision for staff members that they ought to make for themselves.

Celebrate both good and not-so-good decisions. I'm not suggesting that we embarrass people. Instead, I encourage you to create an environment where it is *safe* to talk through things that went well—and those that didn't. Everyone learns through these types of discussions. You will probably need to go first. Seek permission in advance before talking about a decision that another person made. Failing is not the issue—making the same mistake over again is.

Think through the task or project you are delegating, and discuss in advance expectations for feedback and a range of possible solutions. This can be difficult. Total and complete delegation is usually not a wise option. However, do try to explain any and all expectations you have as the leader and give those coordinating the project the opportunity to share their expectations as well. Be honest about any expectations you may have. Sometimes as a leader you really need the person or team to carefully think through solutions and then allow you to give feedback at key points in the process because you can't specifically identify what you want as an outcome. Establish a time sequence for their seeking your feedback. Do *not* wait until a project is completed before giving your feedback—this demoralizes the team. If you have limits to a solution, explain those in advance as well. Discuss budgets, completion dates, and any results that they must ensure are in their recommendations. Also talk about any "political landmines" that might need to be navigated.

If this illness is pervasive in your life, get long-term treatment that includes professional help. If you find that implementing the above-listed solutions is too hard or you just can't seem to make the changes, please face the reality of this illness in your life. You probably need more drastic treatment. Prayerfully consider a soul friend, mentor, or life coach who could help you by providing accountability, wise advice, and a confidential listening ear. Select someone outside of your ministry who you trust and who has the life experience that could assist you in your struggles.

A Final Word

All of us suffer with some level of this malady. Denying the reality of its presence in our lives will only hinder the work that God desires to complete in our lives and in the organizations we serve. We need to face the fact that we are not hiding these symptoms from anyone but ourselves. People love us and will willingly assist us in finding health—but only if we ask for that help. Let's make the decision to serve God to the best of our ability—especially when it means facing and owning our weaknesses.

11

Central Nervous System Disorder

Symptom: when the board and the leadership team are out of sync

This illness occurs when the ruling body of your organization (e.g., elders, deacons) and its senior leaders are out of sync. Usually the results of this malady are considerable: lack of trust, strong differences of opinion, interpersonal conflict, power struggles, pain, and confusion for all involved. You also may experience declining attendance; inability to retain talented staff; lack of mission fulfillment; and loss of focus, passion, or motivation. Many times the organization looks like a malfunctioning, battery-operated stuffed animal—one with limbs flailing around and out of control. It exhibits plenty of intense movement, but none of it is coordinated enough to produce any fruitful results for God's kingdom.

As I thought about an illustration to describe this infirmity, I realized that I could select a story that demonstrates the illness from the senior leader's point of view—or from the elder, deacon, or church board member's point of view. Choosing either approach could result in my slanting the viewpoint in favor of one or the other. Instead, I hope to provide a story that illustrates both viewpoints without overly favoring either group. Even this struggle illustrates a critical component of this illness—an us-versus-them mentality.

Another tension I felt in writing this illustration is the fact that I didn't want to address the extreme form of this disease: unhealthy staff members and churches which have been that way for years. Those churches have long lines of former staff members who were almost destroyed. And the converse is also true: some churches may never fully recover from narcissistic former staff members who used the church for their purposes only—with no regard for the people, mission, or the health of the church. In this chapter I'm not addressing this extreme and fatal form of this illness. Instead, I hope to illustrate that when ruling bodies and staff members are locked in a dance of conflict, they need help pulling themselves back into a healthy approach to ministry.

Major Signs of Illness

The pressures and misunderstandings had been building for months in Luke's spirit. As the senior pastor of a large, multi-ethnic church for the past three years, he had weathered numerous challenges and built a pastoral team that was highly effective, turning the church from a severe downfall in numbers and ministries into a growing, dynamic, and exciting community. Luke understood that over these three years, he had asked the elders to move much quicker and take more risks than they were accustomed to doing. Luke also realized that he had used a lot of his personal "credibility points" with the elders in order to overcome some of the past challenges. Numerous unavoidable factors had made this pace and level of risk necessary. Luke knew that he needed to manage the pace of change for the sake of the church. However, the dire situation and limited time frame warranted this accelerated rate.

The accomplishments of the past three years were indeed astounding. Outside members of the community were elated, and the church was now the subject of much positive talk around town. It had now progressed from having a reputation as being unstable and declining toward being known as a place where God was doing wonderful new things.

However, it seemed that the more effective the senior pastor, associate pastors, and staff became, the more Darrin (the elder board chair) and the other elders concentrated on and pointed out more minor areas that were not fully resolved. The elders appeared unwilling to celebrate the significant things that God was doing. They began pointing out deficiencies in Luke and some of the other pastors. The elders felt justified in their accusations; the pastors felt attacked. An uninvolved observer would quickly note that due to the massive pressures of having to turn the church around quickly, the pastors, staff, and lay leadership of the church had not spent enough relational time together. They hadn't invested enough time personally in *each other* before beginning the actual—and sometimes painful—ministry of the church's transformation.

As a result of these perceived attacks, Luke was confused and hurt, and without consciously realizing it, he subtly began to maneuver the lay leadership to recognize and celebrate the accomplishments of the staff. Though Luke knew and repeatedly emphasized that God deserved all the recognition for the improvement that had occurred over the past three years, he also knew that the pastors and staff had sacrificially and skillfully led the organization to a healthy, new place. Luke wasn't blind to the areas in which each member of his staff needed improvement—nor was he blind to his own weaknesses. However, the successful outcomes of their efforts seemed to demonstrate that they were managing these areas of imperfection well, and the church was on a path for long-term impact in its local community.

Darrin, however, judged that Luke wasn't facing the real issues and challenges of the church. He recognized that Luke's and the other pastors' leadership had made a difference, but he also believed that Luke didn't properly recognize the hard work of the elders. Darrin also thought Luke moved far too quickly and bypassed proper process, asking the elders and lay leadership to act without enough time to reflect and pray. Additionally, he thought that Luke did not adequately honor and receive input from the elders when making decisions. Darrin perceived that instead of listening carefully, Luke was actually manipulating the elders in an attempt to get them to accept his ideas. As a result, Darrin felt unappreciated, undervalued, and disrespected.

Before long, Darrin began to share these concerns with other elders. He discovered that many of the concerns were shared by a small group of elders but not the majority of the board. Soon a coalition—actually small in number but large in influence—of disgruntled elders began to arise. A downward spiral began. The more Darrin tried to draw Luke's attention to what he thought were the real issues of the church and the changes he judged Luke needed to make in his leadership and in other members of the pastoral staff, the more Luke tried to coerce Darrin into focusing on the pastors' accomplishments. Out of frustration, Darrin finally decided to take control. He was determined to show Luke that he had to slow down, recognize the authority of the board, and listen more carefully to input from the elders.

Luke was confused and hurt. As he watched Darrin starting to act in a way that he thought was outside the authority of an elder chair, he was becoming disappointed that other elders didn't intervene. While Luke knew that the majority of elders didn't share Darrin's concerns, he was wavering in this belief. Unfortunately, Darrin was now privately using his role to intimidate Luke into compliance. The more this occurred, the more Luke was bewildered as to why Darrin was so dissatisfied with his and the pastoral staff's leadership. The accomplishments over the past three years—all empowered by God—were more than all of the church's growth in the past twenty-five years. *What was going on?*

Luke started to wonder if the elders subconsciously desired that the pastoral staff *under*function in their responsibilities so the elders could assume the role of rescuers of the church. As a result, Luke unknowingly moved into a cautious and protective mode. No longer trusting Darrin, Luke increasingly acted defensive and protective of himself and the staff. Locked in an argument over "whose perspective was correct," Darrin and Luke slid downward into the malaise of reacting negatively to *whatever* either said or did—sadly, no longer able to believe the best of each other. Their communication deteriorated into a war of words with no attempts to understand the other's perspective. Negatively judging each other's motives, both assumed that no matter what the other did, it was either wrong or done for the wrong reasons.

Before long Luke reached his breaking point: quickly and quietly he found a new church to serve where he hoped the elders would appreciate and support his leadership initiatives. Darrin, feeling vindicated because Luke left, still faced the challenge of explaining Luke's abrupt departure, developing strategies for retaining the church's other talented pastors and staff, and managing the damage control among the members of the congregation and in the community due to the popular senior pastor's departure. While Darrin was sorry that Luke would not make the necessary changes to become the leader that the elders wanted, he was satisfied that the elders were firmly back in control. Darrin was also convinced that they could and would now find a new senior pastor who would follow the lead of the elders rather than leading the church as Luke had.

Cataloging the Signs of Illness

1. Us-versus-them mentality

I don't know where this "fortress mentality" first originated. But over my thirty-one years of vocational ministry, I have observed it and unfortunately acted upon it numerous times. It's usually revealed in comments like this: "Lay leaders will never be able to understand the sacrifice and hard work that it takes to do ministry full time." The reverse comment is: "Those pastors would never make it if they had to actually work for a living in the real world." There are indeed some nuisances that are only fully understood by those who have actually been in a specific role and setting. However, when we start thinking that *no one* ever understands us, then we are probably caught in this mentality.

2. Miscommunication

When you observe that previously effective ways to communicate are now resulting in confusion, you may be suffering from this infirmity. If emails are regularly being misunderstood in ways that they were not before, or if other forms of written communication are no longer effective, consider this diagnosis. Or if you find yourself overanalyzing or being overanalyzed in every word that you write, say, or hear from others, you are probably caught in a downward spiral toward central nervous system disorder. Keeping copies of all forms of correspondence—just in case you need proof for motives or facts—may indicate you have progressed well into this disorder. Note that I'm not talking about keeping good records but about a fear of being continually misunderstood.

3. Power struggles

Spending too much time strategizing ways to outmaneuver another person may signify the presence of this disease. And if you're investing much of your energy and time in trying to predict how that person will act next—so that you're prepared to counterattack—you're in advanced stages of central nervous system disorder. You'll probably also notice that every time you have an idea, this person is opposed. The opposite is also most likely evident: you're opposed to everything that other person suggests. If you can't remember what the original issue really was *because you're so intent on beating the other person at his or her game,* you are indeed very ill.

4. Overly cautious, protective, or mistrusting

It's difficult to fault Luke in the story above for becoming overly cautious or protective. This fallen world has far too many unsafe people, and we're foolish if we allow ourselves to become easy prey for them. Following Jesus's instructions that we be "wise as serpents and harmless as doves" (Matt. 10:16) isn't easy. When we're attacked or misunderstood, we naturally want to fight back or retreat into a protective environment that we can control.

This symptom, however, is about our misguided attempts to *over*-protect in ways that eventually lead to an inordinate amount of mistrust. In this type of situation, resolving conflict in a healthy way isn't seen from the vantage point of a covenant between two people who are committed to each other and to working out their differences for the sake of the organization. Instead, conflict is seen as unhealthy and people's goals are to win at all costs. They may also sever the covenant because they want to prove *I'm right* or *I'm more powerful*. Sadly, the good of the organization becomes lost in this struggle to win.

5. Inability to identify, effectively discuss, and resolve the real issues

Inability to identify the real source, issue, or root of conflict among people is one sign of this infirmity. Unwittingly, those involved become locked in a battle for the sake of fighting alone; they've lost sight of the original issue or the actual issue which is now in front of them. Eventually they spiral down into becoming adversaries who fight over any and all issues.

At one church where I served, we were experiencing a rather large amount of new people joining the church. Many of these people were transfers from other churches in the region; some were leaving their churches because of church fights. So at each new members' class we said something like this: "Some of you may have left a church that was caught up in a church fight. Here, we refuse to encourage a combative atmosphere. Instead, we commit ourselves to seeking forgiveness and to finding ways to serve together in peace. You're most likely unaware of how the discord in your last church may continue to affect you, and this is only natural. So if you have indeed left a church that was in the midst of conflict, we ask that you take around six months to be served by all our services and ministries. This will hopefully give you ample time to heal. Once you have healed, we would love to help you find a place of service here at the church."

6. Lack of Forgiveness

Are you finding it increasingly difficult to forgive and move to a healthier new place? Are you struggling because every time you make the mental decision to forgive the other person, he or she reopens your wounds because of yet another offensive behavior? Or are you discovering that no matter how much you apologize and repent of your wrong behavior, you still seem to be on a discouraging uphill climb to gain the forgiveness of the other person? After a sincere apology and repeated attempts to put things right, is the offended party still rehearsing all your offenses and how poorly he or she was treated? Worse yet, has the other person gone silent and withdrawn from you while he or she recruits others to this cause or offense against you? Do you wish harm or ill of this person? Lastly, are you unable to see *any* good in what the other person says or does? All these are significant symptoms of a lack of forgiveness.

Treatment

Do your best not to feed the monstrous downward spiral of conflict. Conflict can take on a life of its own, quickly turning into unhealthy attacks on other persons or groups. Unhealthy conflict that quickly intensifies can also ruin your ability to stay on track with the original issue; it can rapidly expand to include what might otherwise be trivial issues. As soon as possible, attempt to step away from the conflict, and if you can, retreat to a quiet place where you can prayerfully ask God to give you the wisdom and the strength to break this cycle. Seek counsel from a confidential and wise friend. Ask yourself these questions: How am I contributing to the discord? How might I stop the downward cycle, working instead to get the conflict healthy and productive—not attacking or trying to destroy the other person or group?

In the illustration of Luke and Darrin, one of them needed to step back and find the perspective that would allow both to see how they were contributing to the problem. Neither seemed able to gain any insight into the other person's viewpoint, so they spiraled into an unrelenting tailspin. When one would misinterpret the other's actions or words, they moved ever deeper into the desperate struggle to prove, *I'm the one who's right*. The more Darrin tried to get Luke to see things from his point of view, the more Luke became defensive and attempted to get Darrin to acknowledge his accomplishments. Both fed the downward spiral, allowing the conflict to build to the point of no return.

Decide to seek and grant forgiveness. Even when dealing with an unsafe person—one who requires consequences before forgiveness is granted—we are required to make the mental decision to forgive. Granting and seeking forgiveness comes in stages and requires time. However, requiring that another person prove that he or she has changed or has been punished sufficiently before making the mental decision to grant forgiveness is wrong. The work of healing emotionally and eventually restoring the relationship comes later and will be hard.

Aren't you thankful that God chose to forgive you *before* you proved worthy of his forgiveness? This foundational truth should motivate us all to forgive in the way God does. We need to ask God to reveal how *we* have wronged another person. When seeking forgiveness, we also need to focus on asking, "Will you forgive me?" versus merely saying, "I'm sorry." Embracing your responsibility when hurting another, explaining how you know that you've hurt them, and then asking them to forgive you reflects the biblical approach to forgiveness. Apologies can be shallow and are often only effective with resolving minor or more surface offenses.

Someone has to decide to "become Jesus," but it is best when both parties assume this posture. If this reads like a simple cliche, that is not my intent. Or does it sound like I'm asking you to die for the sake of others? Actually, yes, this may be required. What I hope to convey is a deep understanding that the process of forgiveness almost always involves suffering, sacrifice, death to self, and the firm decision to see another person or group from the vantage point of Jesus—as loved and valued.

Resolving conflict may demand that one person—or even better, both parties—die to themselves. They need to seek a posture of humility and repentance, resolving the conflict for the sake of the organization and, even more importantly, for the kingdom of God. I have personally paid this painful price, and others have paid this cost on my behalf. This is *not* a shallow request to follow Jesus; rather, it is a call to take up his cross and follow him. Quite frankly, I wish that leadership never required this costly price. Only naive leaders fail to understand this inevitable pathway of spiritual leadership. And none easily accept it.

To avoid miscommunication, listen carefully so that you can fully understand the other person or group. Also, reflect on your own words and actions. Ask yourself these questions: How could what I said or did be misunderstood by the other person? What are the ways I might have misunderstood the other person? Again, seek the counsel of a wise and confidential friend to help you gain a more objective understanding of the situation and how you might have misinterpreted conversations and events. Concentrate on asking God to reveal to you *your* offenses instead of focusing on how you have been offended.

Work to understand what real issues initially caused the conflict. Usually when discord erupts, it has been simmering and building for months beforehand. Therefore, prayerfully seek God's help in identifying all the underlying sources. In Darrin and Luke's situation, the feelings and judgments of being unappreciated and not respected grew from their inability to discuss their differing concerns in a healthy manner. If Darrin could have told Luke how much he valued his leadership and found a way to communicate to Luke ways both of them might make changes in order to better serve together, perhaps the story could have ended differently. I wonder what would have happened had Luke told Darrin how much he appreciated him and then expressed understanding of how difficult it was for Darrin to lead the elders at such a fast pace. If Luke could have offered his ideas on how the two of them could lead the church and the elders at a more sustainable and agreeable pace, would Luke and Darrin still be serving together? Regardless, we all need to utilize the principle that effective conflict resolution begins with a comprehensive understanding of the core issues.

Try to remove yourself from the power struggle. This is difficult and takes a sustained commitment, but you're better off focusing on the positive changes that you could make in the way you're responding or leading in this situation (though they may be difficult or not your preference). Commit to making those changes. Do your best not to react to the other person's attempts to show you "who's the boss." Be humble, be wise, and don't fall into any traps that the other person may place in your path.

In the previous story, Darrin started to look for and document evidence that Luke was overstepping his level of authority. Darrin wanted to prove to the other elders how difficult Luke was to work with. Faced with this situation, Luke needed to slow down, not introduce any unnecessary changes, listen more carefully, and ensure that he didn't act without proper elder input. Luke needed to assure Darrin—verbally and with his actions—that he would submit to the leadership of the elders. This could have taken a long time and potentially been extremely frustrating for Luke, but it might have diffused the power struggles, resulting in a resolution of the conflict.

Find ways to rebuild trust. Maintaining trust is always easier than rebuilding it. Many liken trust to a bank account: it takes a lot to build the balance—and very little to deplete the account. Rebuilding broken trust will take time and commitment over a sustained period. And unfortunately, there are no shortcuts! The work begins with seeking and granting forgiveness; you must then be faithful and diligent in making the necessary changes. If Luke and Darrin could have found some positive means to resolve their differences, they next would have needed to covenant together to develop and implement strategies to ensure that this didn't occur again. Unfortunately, in their case, this never happened.

Remember the differences between healthy and unhealthy conflict. Healthy conflict operates within a covenant that understands that when conflict occurs, everyone works to resolve the conflict for the good of the organization. Healthy conflict takes place when everyone seeks to understand and assist each other in finding positive resolution. In contrast, unhealthy conflict means working from a contract basis—one that can easily be broken and involves fighting to win or to prove who is right. Paying no attention to the needs of the organization, those locked in unhealthy conflict focus on attacking, punishing, or destroying the other person. They may also use lies, spread rumors and gossip, and attempt to damage the reputation of another. Most importantly, even when you're facing unhealthy conflict, commit to being healthy in how *you* respond. And lastly, remember to be wise—not naive.

A Final Word

No healthy person enjoys conflict. Yet servants of Christ know that conflict is inevitable and that they must effectively lead through conflict. The key question is, how will you and your organization turn that conflict into a healthy process, seeking the best results possible? Many have said that "peace at all costs is too costly" because you will never reach peace and instead will only discover more conflict. Therefore, absence of conflict is not our goal; rather, we should be doing all we can to keep conflict healthy and productive while building flourishing organizations within the kingdom of God.

12

Conjunctivitis

Symptom: an attitude that volunteers are not
dependable

Many vocational staff members confidentially assume
as fact that volunteers are not fully dependable and cannot be trusted to handle the most important leadership
tasks in the organization. They tend to cling even more
tightly to this belief when a limit is placed on hiring more
full-time staff. The thought behind this is that volunteers
are just too busy, not motivated enough, and not accountable enough to be expected to complete their responsibilities at a level equal to that of a paid staff member.
When paid staff members believe and subconsciously
act upon these assumptions, unpaid staff members can
sense these expectations. This usually results in an organization's most dependable unpaid staff either choosing
not to serve or being poorly mobilized, to the detriment
of the organization and the kingdom of God.

Major Signs of Illness

The concept of involving lay church members in doing ministry is not new or even unrecognized. In fact, most pastors know within their first week of vocational ministry that they can't possibly do all the work of the church by themselves or secure enough funds to pay all the needed workers. They know and firmly believe the truth from Ephesians 4—that believers must be equipped for works of service, not works of sitting and watching pastors do the ministry—but they are sometimes baffled by how to move church members from being ministry-*watchers* to becoming fully equipped ministry-*doers*. Fortunately, a number of national parachurch ministries are focused on guiding pastors and church leadership teams toward refocusing their congregations to help every member minister in some meaningful way.

But beyond the traditional roles of Sunday school teachers, choir members, and deacons, just how much responsibility can a "volunteer" really handle? (The very term *volunteer* seems incongruent with God's desire that *all* of his people engage in acts of service in his name. Doesn't that make us *all* God's staff? I prefer the terminology *unpaid staff*.) Sure, they can be trusted to pour the punch at youth events, drive vans to nursing home ministries, or even organize the vacation Bible school. But what about the "really important stuff"—the kinds of work for which, in our *sophisticated* churches, it seems safer to hire or contract with professionals to do for us? Surely God didn't include the *hard* stuff among the acts of service that he desires lay leaders to undertake?

A friend who served for several years as the director of equipping ministries in a large church worked hard to help the congregation progress in their understanding of involving lay people in the work of the ministry. Ministries began to grow and flourish as more members joined in the work and grew passionate about serving. Then along came a crucial time in the life of the church: the need for an extensive capital campaign. When my friend was asked to organize the church's capital campaign, she was advised that one of her first tasks would be to choose and hire the fundraising firm that would design and publish the campaign promotional materials. Within weeks her mailbox was stuffed with mailings from companies and organizations with marketing expertise, all offering competitive rates for their services. She began to narrow down the choices and determine which professional firm might be the best and most affordable match.

Yet something seemed wrong. She thought, if the church really believed that the people of God should be about doing the work of the ministry, why would the church invest significant funds in hiring a company to do what its own members could do? Was it too risky to ask church members to commit to volunteering at a professional level of skill? Or was it instead a step of faith to ask God's direction for building a team of people who would commit to this huge task as their work of service? After several conversations and much prayer about the risk involved, the pastoral leadership team was persuaded to see if indeed God's people could be trusted to carry out a project that was professional in nature.

A search ensued to find those in the congregation who might have backgrounds or careers in writing, marketing, designing, and publishing, as well as a dedication to serving God through their skills and talents. Each person chosen readily signed on for this experiment and seemed to clearly understand the importance of the task ahead. All of the team members seemed energized by the size of the responsibility being assigned to them! Eagerly they set to work, and within a few weeks they had successfully created a campaign theme and logo and designed multiple materials to be used church-wide to explain the campaign. One team member who owned a small publishing company willingly printed the materials at cost. The results: through this work done entirely by committed, skilled members, the church saved many thousands of dollars while still creating high-quality campaign materials for distribution.

The people who served on the team were changed through the time they invested in praying over their decisions and work, as well as through their new commitment to the campaign itself. Perhaps most importantly, the church's pastors and leaders gained a new level of understanding and experience in what God can do through his people who are equipped for works of service.

Cataloging the Signs of Illness

1. Inability to recruit sufficient levels of unpaid staff

When you struggle to recruit enough unpaid staff to complete ministry programs within your church, you may suffer from this illness. Unpaid staff members can easily ascertain whether they are respected or distrusted by the way they're treated. Usually paid staff members initially communicate this in the way they recruit. They mistakenly think that making the job appear easy and lowering expectations will improve their recruiting efforts. In reality, the opposite is true: these paid staff members inadvertently send the message that unpaid staff positions aren't really important. Who wants to invest their limited time and resources serving in positions that aren't important—or so that others can get on with the important things? Not me!

2. The most talented members of your church aren't willing to assume unpaid staff positions within your organization

This symptom differs from the previous point because it focuses on *ability* rather than just *number* of unpaid staff. When paid staff believe that unpaid staff members aren't trustworthy, it becomes a self-fulfilling prophecy: the most talented members of your organization will not serve where their talents aren't appreciated and mobilized. You may be thinking that these talented people are being selfish and should simply serve where you want them to because it helps your organization. If so, then I need to make this more plain: What is your spiritual gift? What are you passionate about? What do you enjoy doing that refreshes and recharges your spirit, enabling you to do more in the kingdom of God? Now, *imagine what would happen if you spent the majority of your time as a paid staff member doing things of little personal interest to you or that you judge are not that important.* Apply those same thoughts and feelings to unpaid staff members. Still convinced they ought to relent and serve where you want to put them?

3. Extremely high dropout rates among unpaid staff

We tend to think that high dropout rates among unpaid staff members are normal and to be expected because we've made the positions too difficult. Usually this is not the case. In my experience and opinion, high dropout rates are due to poor support from the paid staff members who recruited them or to paid staff not taking them seriously enough. Yes, too large a job can overwhelm anyone—either paid or unpaid staff. We need to push the standard high but be realistic when recruiting. However, high dropout rates among unpaid staff probably point to the existence of this malady within your organization rather than an intrinsic deficiency in your unpaid staff.

4. Tired and overwhelmed paid staff

Leading unpaid staff will take time and energy from already busy schedules and lists of what can appear to be endless responsibilities. In light of this workload, many times paid staff members will use the excuse that they just don't have the time to recruit, train, and supervise all these unpaid staff. These excuses are real and understandable in their minds, but they are unacceptable. Once the transitional phase of treating this illness is over, most staff find that their responsibilities have indeed changed—but *not* increased—due to supervising unpaid staff. Also, when paid staff members view hiring more paid staff as the only answer to their weariness and need to get more accomplished, they're afflicted with conjunctivitis. Allowing this excuse to continue endangers the health of your organization.

5. Inability or unwillingness to move from "star" to "player coach"

Tracey was a gifted leader in our young adult ministry. Her abilities to connect with people as a passionate and insightful communicator were extraordinary. Soon numerous other gifted young adults joined this ministry, and it quickly grew to over one hundred consistent attendees. Her young adult ministry was the place to be. Unfortunately, her talent as a speaker could only take the ministry to a certain level of effectiveness. So eventually these other highly talented young adults discovered that the ministry was solely about Tracey's teaching, but she didn't possess the ability to mobilize them into significant leadership positions within the ministry. As usually happens when this occurs, large numbers of guests came and stayed for a while, but an equally large number of regular attendees left because they desired to serve in significant ways.

When I confronted Tracey with these problems, her only solution was to declare that actually I was the problem. She claimed this was true because I wouldn't give her sufficient funds to hire more paid staff to do the other pressing needs so that she could be freed to spend all her time studying and teaching. When I reminded her of the biblical mandate for leaders to mobilize others into ministry, her first reaction was to insist, "I didn't sign on to supervise unpaid staff, and I don't have the slightest idea how to do that." Later I'll discuss how Tracey and I worked through this impasse.

Treatment

Start by personally and consistently modeling your commitment to this value. If you are asking your staff to mobilize unpaid staff members and you aren't modeling this value, you will not find relief from this sickness. Ask yourself some key questions: Are there some important spots in your area of responsibilities where unpaid staff members can assume a role? Are your actions and words consistently modeling the importance of treating this malady? How are you building relationships with unpaid staff members and recruiting them for other areas within your organization in addition to your area? Are you keeping the most talented staff for your personal ministry areas? How often do you discuss this and share your successes and failures in implementing treatment for this infirmity?

Patiently and persistently provide training for all staff on how to effectively recruit and mobilize unpaid staff. Only recently have seminaries started to provide training in this area. Many paid staff—whether seminary trained or not—don't know how to lead this type of initiative. Numerous ministries exist that can provide excellent training and resources for you to utilize in training staff members. Schedule repeated training seminars and provide coaching for staff members who struggle with how to make this work in their particular ministry areas. Include a thorough discussion on why and how the focus and roles of the paid staff members need to adapt in order to successfully implement this new initiative. Incorporate the biblical mandates for Christian leaders to lead by mobilizing others—rather than being the stars themselves. At the same time, be sensitive to the insecurity that occurs when people are asked to make changes in how they do ministry. Everyone needs to know that they can successfully accomplish the required changes and will be given ample time and support to make these changes happen.

In Tracey's story above, this proved to be a key solution. Once she realized that we were serious about this new direction and that we would provide ample training and coaching, she started to slowly change. When Tracey began implementing some of these changes, she personally observed how properly mobilized unpaid staff would actually allow her to make more time for her study and teaching. With time and lots of encouragement and insistence, eventually Tracey discovered that supervising unpaid staff became a valued part of her responsibilities that also freed her to be an even more effective teacher. She also realized that she could train other unpaid teachers to teach periodically, giving her even more time to prepare. Granted, not all of these situations turn out this way. I've had to release paid staff because even after being given proper time and support to adapt, they still refused.

Consistently expect your paid staff to mobilize unpaid staff. Treating this disease takes time. Attempts at quick miracle cures will only fail to eliminate the full illness and will inhibit paid staff in responding to further treatment. Make mobilizing unpaid staff members a component in annual reviews of all paid staff. Using compensation as an incentive will clearly communicate how important this value is to your organization, but tell staff in advance. Hold yourself and all paid staff accountable to implement these changes. Have other staff tell the success stories that they are experiencing; this makes the change initiative appear realistic and possible. Consider a freeze on hiring any new paid staff members until the leaders of a particular department demonstrate that they are mobilizing unpaid staff effectively and that the unfilled position truly warrants a new paid staff member.

Treat unpaid staff with respect and raise your expectations of their performance rather than lowering them. Who wants to serve where little is expected? Granted, some positions within your organization may indeed require more commitment than skill—like the nursery. Please don't get mad at me for using that example! Yes, it takes skill to change diapers, implement proper security measures, and make babies happy. However, it doesn't call for a lot of creativity, training, or talent to be a successful nursery worker. When recruiting an unpaid staff member for a position within your organization, first explain why this ministry position is important to the mission of the organization. Describe expectations for performance and list support and resources that will be available to the person assuming leadership. Also explain the reporting structure and how that person and his or her supervisor will know that the unpaid staff member has been successful. You might even consider implementing a ninety-day review, six-month review, and twelve-month review. On subsequent years, use an annual review process. Enlist all unpaid staff members for a one-year commitment, to be reviewed and renewed if both the unpaid staff member and supervisor agree. And finally, tell your unpaid staff members that the positions they will hold are so important to the ministry that you will expect them to complete their responsibilities successfully.

Allow the pain of being understaffed to exist, and even consider increasing the pain for staff members who fail to implement treatment. This may include not replacing paid positions when paid staff members leave, lowering annual merit raises, passing someone over for promotion, and eventually asking someone to leave. Treating this illness is so important that even the most gifted paid staff star performer may need to be replaced in order to reach the biblical imperatives for Christian leaders. Remember to follow the principles for replacing staff as explained in previous chapters. Keep your standards consistent all across the ministry. All paid staff—regardless of position—must learn to mobilize unpaid staff as one of their top priorities.

At times mobilize unpaid staff to positions that are greater than your organization can offer. Hector was a young, talented, former CEO who had retired early, was independently wealthy, and was looking for a place to live out his passion for leading teams to accomplish extremely large-scale and difficult things in God's kingdom. I wanted desperately to find a place within our church where he could lead. We needed his leadership and resources. Yet I knew that while we were accomplishing some wonderful things within God's mission for us as a church, Hector had global leadership potential. It was a difficult decision and process when I finally realized that my job was to assist Hector by introducing him to the leader of another organization that had the exact opening for Hector's skills and passion. Hector stayed as a member of our church and gave generously, and God continued to use him in a powerful way on a global scale. I wish I could say that it was easy for me to release Hector to serve at another organization, but it wasn't. I'm convinced, however, that God's kingdom was better served because I didn't limit my thinking and stand in the way of God's plans for Hector.

When hiring future paid staff, ensure that they are free of this malady. Hiring paid staff that are already free of this disease and embrace mobilizing unpaid staff members as a way to enhance God's ministry remains the best way to treat this illness. When interviewing potential paid staff members, ask them to demonstrate how they have mobilized unpaid staff in their previous ministry positions. Have them explain how they recruited and supervised unpaid staff. Look for clear evidence of their embracing this value.

A Final Word

Building and leading a team of paid and unpaid staff members requires commitment, persistence, skill, and wisdom. Ironically, the biggest obstacles to mobilizing unpaid staff members are the paid staff members themselves. Remember that it will take time and considerable effort and resources to successfully treat staff conjunctivitis. As I review the biblical teachings on the role and responsibilities of shepherd-leaders, I can't ignore God's requirement that we equip others for work in God's kingdom. It is so much bigger than ourselves.

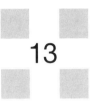

13

Rigidity of the Body

Symptom: too fixed in one place to budge—even an
   inch

   This illness expresses itself in a clinched jaw, tightened
fist, iron will, deaf ear, and total inability to accept any
suggestions from others—let alone implement changes.
Those suffering from this potentially terminal malady
believe that they "have it all figured out" to the most
minute details; they're fully convinced that their program
or ministry is the best in your organization and has been
for years. No changes need to be offered or considered
because they've already made any decisions that will ever
need to be made. Many times a long line of discarded
bodies lies along the landscape of the past years of this
ministry. These are the bodies of those who endeavored
to offer or persisted to suggest that changes needed to
occur. Some readers may suggest that this really isn't an
infection but instead a deadly virus. I concur.

Major Signs of Illness

In many ways, Mark and Nancy were ideal lay leaders in our church—they were passionate about the ministry they led; worked tirelessly; contributed many hours in their shared leadership role; and lived their rather public, "on a pedestal" lives with apparent relative ease. Early in the church's growth they had recognized the need for a particular ministry to adults in the congregation and had taken the initiative and responsibility to develop it into an effective outreach to newcomers that had thrived for years. The dedicated couple had stepped up to take ownership of the ministry—in itself, a good thing. However, they had gradually taken so much ownership that the ministry no longer belonged to the church or even to the Lord. Instead, it was *theirs*.

As long as no one disagreed with or questioned Mark and Nancy, they served for years with what appeared to be joyful hearts and willing spirits. But as more years passed, major changes occurred in three areas of the church: the needs of the congregation as a whole; the needs of individuals served by their ministry; and the preferred direction of the senior leadership of the church. As the incongruity became ever more apparent, one fact became ever more clear: Mark and Nancy would *not* allow change to happen on their watch. Where once their hearts were focused upon the needs of the people they served, gradually their focus had changed to a strong-willed, hold-the-fortress mentality that shut out all ideas from the pastors and other lay leaders. Yet they continued on.

The first time Mark and Nancy raised a complaint about Pam, the staff person who was assigned to provide administrative support for them, I concluded that although Pam was serving others very competently, perhaps her personality just didn't mesh well with Mark and Nancy. I therefore reassigned Pam, assuming all parties involved would be more satisfied if she were to assist other ministries instead. By the time I learned of Mark and Nancy's discontent with Fern, the person newly assigned to replace Pam, they had already reduced her to tears, and she had quickly found employment elsewhere. Fern didn't tell us of the conflict until afterward because, based on her inability to please them, she had quickly concluded that she wasn't suited for working in a church at all.

At this point you may already be asking yourself, *Why weren't Mark and Nancy asked to step down?* Because they had served and led so visibly for so long, to rock their boat would be to ride some stormy seas of our own. Also, they were close personal friends of many influential members of the church, and they were major donors. So instead of taking more drastic measures, we prayed, hoped, searched for, and finally hired yet another assistant.

A brief honeymoon ensued, and we could tell ourselves for a while longer that perhaps this had just been a personality conflict all along. Mark and Nancy loved Lucy's work and hailed her as a wonderful asset to their ministry—but only for a few months. Then came the day when they arrived at my office red-faced and demanding to see me about a very serious matter. You guessed it: Lucy. Mark reported that despite his very clear and repeated direction, Lucy had ignored his wishes and persisted in running this ministry *her way* and must receive disciplinary correction—if not be fired immediately.

This description didn't seem to fit Lucy, and we'd had no other complaints about her work. Trying to discover what had happened, I asked, "Before I intervene, can you provide an example of a time when Lucy has followed her own path rather than your leadership in this ministry?"

Mark's brow furrowed into deep lines, and his wife's face reddened even more. "I certainly can," he bellowed, "for it happened just today." He waved a sheaf of papers in my direction. "Do you see these handouts that I asked Lucy to copy for tonight's meeting? Well, she has made them *yellow* when everyone knows that I've always had these handouts printed in *BLUE!* I tell you, I will not tolerate this insubordination!"

The disease of rigidity of the body was now running rampant. I knew it would hurt many more unsuspecting parts of the body if not stopped. I wish I had a success story to share about treating this illness, but unfortunately, I never did develop a workable plan. All my attempts failed miserably, resulting in major conflict within the church. Bolstered by their financial status and long-standing membership in the church, Mark and Nancy were successful in quickly marshalling support from other leaders within the church and telling just enough of the story to make it appear as though they'd been treated unfairly. *Nothing* I tried worked.

Unfortunately, my attempts to treat this illness resulted in my losing a large amount of credibility as one of the senior leaders. Paid and unpaid staff members knew the damage Mark and Nancy's leadership had produced over the years; however, they also knew that I was unable to adequately find the right solutions. The result was that now they quietly wondered about my ability to lead the staff, period.

Soon I also lost the support of the senior leader, which meant that Mark and Nancy were allowed to continue in their positions. The senior leader knew all of their past history, but he couldn't bring himself to accept the solution that this couple should leave. He hoped that we could fix this impasse and make it simply go away by reassigning them to another department within the church, having them report to one of my colleagues instead of me, and once again hiring a new staff person to assist them. As you would expect, the problems didn't dissipate. Not until four years later, and through the diligent help of another staff pastor, did this illness finally reach a point where the senior pastor and influential lay leaders could no longer endure the damage of Mark and Nancy's leadership.

Given this story, a very legitimate question at this point would be, "If you failed, Craig, then how can you help *me* figure out how to treat this illness?" Truthfully, I'm not positive I can. However, I want to offer the strength of my looking back, sharing the lessons I learned in treating this potentially terminal illness.

Hopefully, I can also model the truth that even with the most prayerfully thought-through strategies and the precise implementation of those strategies, not all staff problems will go well. Our cultural sense of justice fools us into thinking that all problems have a good solution, and that it's just a matter of finding the right answer. The reality is that in this fallen world, some problems will be solved only when Christ our Lord returns.

Cataloging the Signs of Illness

1. Inability to positively receive and accept suggestions

Many times this illness expresses itself as a belief that "No one could improve on my program or ministry." In its worst forms, it's the belief that "People are attacking *my* abilities as a leader when they offer suggestions." Anyone offering a suggestion can easily be seen as an enemy or as a person who "just doesn't understand how effective this ministry has been over the past years." The question of "How could people possibly provide any valuable suggestions?" may be lurking in the minds of those afflicted with rigidity of the body.

2. Frequent mention of old stories concerning how effective this ministry has been

This symptom refers to the retelling of stories that may at first appear recent, but once the teller is pressed, you find out that the success testimonials occurred years ago. Occasionally accompanying this symptom are derogatory references to people of today and how uncommitted or disloyal they are. This is a veiled attempt to blame others for diminishing positive results from the ministry. Failing to accept that the ministry is not as effective as it once was and that it's in need of changes, those suffering from this disease blame others as a way to deflect any possibility of their own ineffectiveness.

3. Inability to separate one's worth as a person from the role as leader of a ministry

This symptom is sad to observe. Basically, those experiencing this infirmity are so defined by their leadership of this ministry that any suggestion is seen as an attack on their worth as a person or leader. Riddled with numerous insecurities and many times failures in other areas of their lives, they control even the smallest details of their decisions because they can't face the risk of change that may mean a loss of security or control. If they can control everything in their ministry, then they can feel good about themselves and ensure their success.

This symptom is always followed with an increasingly strong denial and redefinition of reality. No amount of objective evidence will convince them of the benefits of change, and no amount of positive affirmation will enable them to receive treatment for this illness. Unfortunately, the ministry long ago stopped being about God and the good of the organization. Their needs as leaders of the ministry have now supplanted those motives. It's now all about them.

4. Manipulative attempts to gain your support or friendship in order to solidify the continuance of their ministry

This sign of the malady reveals itself in many different forms. One is the "hidden agenda." When communicating with these people, they generally seem to disguise the *real* reasons they're talking to you. When requesting a meeting, they may offer one reason and then when you meet, before long a totally different topic emerges.

Alicia exhibited a vivid example of this symptom. She would frequently stop me in the hall and ask a quick, innocent-sounding question. I would later hear from another staff member that Alicia had quoted me as saying something entirely different. Strangely, *her* versions of our conversations always seemed to be used to give the appearance that she had my full support in whatever she was requesting.

One of our first quick hallway conversations occurred when she stated how much she valued my wisdom. She wondered if I thought we should provide food for college kids who were at the church volunteering their time to assist us with a time-consuming task. Without thinking carefully, I responded positively and suggested that we order pizza or some other cheap menu item. To my surprise, two hours later the facilities director was outside my office, clearly upset and strongly requesting a meeting. He immediately demanded that I explain why I had overridden his decision to hold the lunch for the college kids in the gym rather than the guest parlor—a beautifully appointed parlor where we did not allow food. To my utter amazement, Alicia had twisted our conversation and told him that I supported her moving the meal to the parlor!

Another form of this malady is the "best friend image." In this case, the disease shows itself when people try to manipulate others into thinking that you and they are best friends. In this way they hope to leverage the appearance of friendship into some form of power for the sake of their ministry. Usually you're alerted to this when other staff members say to you, "I know that you and Alicia are close friends, but I still need to ask you . . ." Or when the infected people give the appearance of being close friends with other influential people within your organization. They hope to hinder your attempts to interfere with their ministry by making you think these other influential people will come to their aid if you don't support *them*.

5. Subtle reminders of one's long-term service, important status in the church, or amount of financial contribution

Those ill with this disease seek to artfully remind you of their importance or position in the church. They may also try to use any means possible to enslave you into supporting *their* decisions and *their* ministries.

When raising funds for the new campus of the seminary, we made the decision not to sell the naming rights to any buildings. Instead, we worked to solicit financial support through prayerful and cogent requests. After many had made their contributions, a committee then decided how their giving to the campaign would be honored. I'm pleased to say that this worked tremendously well. All our donors seemed to give out of purely gracious hearts and to sacrificially enhance the mission of the seminary. What a wonderful environment we've been blessed with rather than settings where donors use their gifts to leverage greater recognition, power, or position within an organization!

6. Numerous former paid or unpaid staff members who served with these people are now reassigned or no longer with your organization

A solution that limits conflict and produces a win for everyone is a desirable goal in most situations. Certainly no healthy person enjoys dealing with conflict! When trying to bring resolution and peace to contention, most people want to ensure that everyone can stay actively involved in the organization. Therefore, reassigning people to other departments, for example, is not a bad idea. But when numerous reassignments and departures occur, these are signs that your organization is ill with this disease.

Treatment

Prayerfully and carefully assess the situation. This illness may only be treatable with fervent prayer, fasting, and the clearly defined support of the senior leader and other influential lay leaders of the organization. You'll need to ask yourself numerous questions, including: Is this the right time to deal with this illness (we'll look at this question more later). Has it become widespread, damaging morale and other ministries? To what degree? Can I wait, allowing God more time to deal with this himself? Do I really have the full support of the necessary supervisors and influential people within the organization? Have I tested the actual level of their support by asking them (1) how they would deal with this and (2) whether they're prepared for these people to multiply the conflict, work to discredit the leaders, or leave the organization? If the supervisors and influential leaders aren't ready to go to that extent, how far are they willing to go with their support? Who knows about the clear history and facts of this situation? Are they influential and willing to stand with me by documenting or sharing these details with my supervisor? How far am I willing to take this? How critical is treatment of this illness at this time?

These are just a few of the essential questions you must repeatedly ask yourself before acting. As a general principle, proceed more slowly than you judge necessary until you are absolutely certain of your next step.

Never tackle this disease alone! Immediately seek confidential counsel from your supervisor, your senior leader, and a trusted third party in the organization. Treating this illness can be fatal to *your* health and position in the church. Ensure that you have an army of supporters willing to coach you through this struggle, even and especially when it gets extremely intense. Ascertain if treating this disease is critical to the long-term health of your organization.

If appropriate, involve the assistance of your organization's governing body. When this illness involves lay leaders, asking the elders, deacons, or board members to take the lead in treatment may be the wisest approach. In that way the governing body can stand up and protect the administrative leaders of the organization. In the organization where my example occurred, the board would never have assumed this role because all staff issues were to be handled by the senior administrators. I can't help but wonder if that contributed to my failure.

When actually confronting those afflicted with this virus, always include an objective and trusted third party who will be seen as very influential by those whom you're confronting. This may seem backwards and illogical, but I warn you, don't involve any third party who's not in the chain of people that the ill parties will potentially use to gather support. Choose someone up the ladder in influence and prestige among the members of your organization. Remember that we're not talking about treating a common sore throat. Instead, we're discussing how to treat a potentially fatal infection that could result in major conflict.

Document everything you can. Choose a few examples of the diseased behavior and then run these by one or preferably two other confidential and objective third parties. Ask them if these examples seem grievous enough to warrant the action you're considering. If not, then either improve your documentation's accuracy or wait until more information emerges. *Never* slant, intensify, or alter the details of the offenses in any manner—no matter how tempting that may be. The documentation *must* be verifiable through multiple sources and able to withstand a microscopic examination.

Ensure that all your sources, supervisors, and appropriate influential people are determined to follow this through and will not retreat if attacked. Ask them how committed they are to seeing this situation healed. Remember that they're probably a little less committed than they appear when you're talking with them.

After your supervisors and sources have had time to reflect, ask them again about their level of commitment to determine if any deterioration of support is occurring. If you sense a waning of support, step back and ask yourself if that waning suggests that you should delay treatment. If in doubt, wait until you're positive that your supervisors and influential people are ready to proceed. Learn from one of my mistakes: I was certain that I had the appropriate support of the senior leader, but I was wrong in my assumption. He withdrew his support almost immediately because of the intense conflict that occurred, even though I had implemented the exact strategy he and I had mutually determined to use.

Have predetermined solutions and exit strategies in place. This was another failure on my part. Specifically, my strategy did not include well-thought-through, multiple solutions and an escape for all parties involved that would have allowed all of us to save face if things went bad. When I confronted Mark and Nancy—by myself—I did not expect their immediate and intense attack on me and my character. In retrospect, I should have seen the assault coming. Also, when I confronted them, I didn't offer possible solutions. Instead, I assumed that they would go home, think through the problems, and then return to my office where we would develop a plan for making changes. Again, these were all the wrong strategies.

Immediately upon leaving my office, they walked directly to the senior leader's office. He was out of town at the time, but they found a way to contact him and then forcibly attacked me and the procedure I used to confront them, and they reminded him of their influence within the organization. Their threats to leave if the senior leader didn't take their side in this argument unnerved the senior leader. Since I had met with them alone, I had no witnesses to my side of the conversation. The sad reality was that now the "score" was two to one.

Next they had another influential member of the organization—a wealthy personal friend—contact the senior leader the same day, also threatening to leave the church if he didn't get me under control. This threat from two major donors was more than the senior leader could withstand—let alone having this critical situation occur on his time away. Now clearly *I* was the problem. Mark and Nancy had successfully diverted the focus from their leadership skills to my supposed unwarranted attacks on them and their ministry. They convinced everyone that it was a personality conflict between them and me rather than a shortcoming in their leadership skills.

I had no way to manage the conflict and refocus the conversation because I had offered no solutions or escape mechanisms. I was standing on the thin ice of one solution alone—their stepping down as leaders. In retrospect, I should have brainstormed with the senior leader a couple of agreeable interim solutions that would show him and others that I was attempting to be reasonable and fair. Possible solutions could have included asking Mark and Nancy to assemble a team of leaders to serve as the decision-making team for their ministry or gaining Mark and Nancy's permission to brainstorm with them ideas that might help their ministry before discarding others' suggestions. Offering Mark and Nancy another place of leadership within the church might have been another possible solution.

Truthfully, I don't believe that any of these would have worked with Mark and Nancy. But they would have proved to the senior leader and others that I was attempting to do all that I could to support Mark and Nancy in finding reasonable solutions to the criticisms that were occurring. These interim solutions also could have been used by the senior leader when explaining the situation to other influential members of the church.

Unfortunately, my lack of perception and wisdom allowed Mark and Nancy to portray themselves as innocent, harmless, and deeply wounded servants of Christ. They accused me of trying to angrily push them out of the ministry they had sacrificially given their lives to lead. Their friends flocked to their support, and my support from supervisors and sources melted away. I was left with little support or momentum.

The senior leader was trapped in a corner with no room to maneuver. If he and I had anticipated these tactics by Mark and Nancy and had agreed beforehand on some interim solutions or escape routes, he wouldn't have been forced to choose between supporting me (and losing his credibility with some influential donors) or supporting Mark and Nancy. Not surprisingly, he took the path of least resistance—buying some time in hopes the conflict would take care of itself. He reassigned Mark and Nancy to report to another staff supervisor and authorized the search for a new staff member to assist them. And then we were right back to the blue paper caper.

I was now wounded and unsure how to recover my credibility among staff and other influential members of the community. My relationship with the senior pastor was strained, and I needed time to retreat and reflect, allowing my wounds to heal. One thing was for sure: Mark and Nancy had won, and their newly found support empowered them in their belief that *no one* was going to tell them what was best for their ministry.

It may be best to allow the ministry to run its course in hopes that the organization will not suffer permanent damage and the virus will eventually go away. You also might seek this solution in hopes that God will resolve the issue directly himself.

Reflecting back on this personal failure is still painful, and I'm profoundly aware of how God protected and healed me. I wonder if allowing the ministry to die a slow death would've been the wiser path. If the senior leader and I had decided to allow Mark and Nancy's ministry to proceed with decreasing support from the church, would we have found a more successful conclusion? If I'd decided to let the illness get so bad that no one could continue to ignore the need for treatment, might I have been able to succeed under those conditions? Or would that have carelessly endangered the overall health of the church? It appeared to me that the ministry was just too important to the church to allow it to continue to decrease in effectiveness.

Many leaders suggest that "addition is a far better path to change than subtraction." Starting a parallel ministry to eventually supplant Mark and Nancy's might have worked, but probably not. It most likely would have been too confusing to church members.

So now it's *your* turn to decide. Is it best to intervene or not, even if you're unsure that a workable solution will be reached?

A Final Word

I wish I could more confidently offer workable solutions for treating this potentially fatal illness. I can't. Instead, I hope I have offered some insightful methods for *designing* treatment. Remember to begin treatment only when you're certain that everyone is committed to seeing it through, the disease is widespread and damaging to the health of your organization, documentation is clear and irrefutable, and lastly, you're in a solid position of leadership with strong credibility. Treating this malady may require several attempts at treatment—somewhat like using multiple courses of antibiotics to heal potentially fatal infections. In the end, perhaps I didn't actually fail but my attempt was simply one necessary initial course of an antibiotic that needed to be followed by later forms of treatment. With Mark and Nancy's illness, this was certainly true.

My prayer is that God will empower and guide you. Not every staff infection has a complete and total cure, but no matter how potentially fatal, they still demand treatment. Proceed with caution.

14

Blocked Carotid Arteries

Symptom: when the supervisor is the problem

You'll quickly recognize the major symptoms of this illness if your supervisor can't seem to make timely decisions, changes decisions too frequently and without warning, doesn't communicate adequately, can't understand or appreciate how much time and effort it takes for you to complete your tasks, leads everything in a crisis mode, and just doesn't want or have the skills to lead but lacks the courage to admit it. You find yourself wishing that your supervisor would just sit down with you, take the time to organize the work, and then stay with the plan. This illness doesn't include immoral, unethical, or other improper actions by the supervisor. Instead, we'll focus on the forms of this illness that can be improved by implementing a few key strategies. If you generally enjoy your role and your supervisor but wish that your supervisor could make some improvements, you'll find helpful suggestions in this chapter.

Major Signs of Illness

I don't remember how I got roped into the job, but I found myself in front of over one hundred administrative assistants, leading a discussion on how they could effectively support, encourage, redirect (yes, *redirect*), and confront their supervisors. While some elements of the conversation were intense, I was amazed at how positive and committed the assistants were to their supervisors. They wanted answers from each other and from me to some of the common challenges they faced in order to help them more successfully complete their duties and assist their supervisors. As I listened, I realized that they wanted to be valued and respected partners in helping their supervisors and organizations be successful.

That discussion resulted in a list of practical methods to use in managing your boss. And if you're questioning the use of the word *manage*, understand that within any organization that has multiple paid or unpaid staff members, you do need to wisely manage all your relationships—with those to whom you report, your peers or colleagues, and lastly, those who report to you. Needless to say, I returned to my office much more aware of how my abilities as a supervisor can positively or negatively affect the work of those who serve with me.

In this chapter I hope to offer some practical suggestions for all paid and unpaid staff members who work with a supervisor. Again, I won't be addressing "terminal" forms of this illness. Rather, I'll focus on improvements for those who basically enjoy their supervisors, accept that their supervisors aren't going to make major changes, and need ideas to help their organizations run more smoothly.

Cataloging the Signs of Illness

1. Not enough valuable communication

This symptom takes on many varying forms. One is the logistical problem of not sharing in a timely fashion information which could have assisted you in completing your tasks. For example, you may have been working on a task in the agreed-upon manner when you heard new information from others or from your supervisor—information that would've saved a lot of time and effort if you'd only known sooner. But because you didn't, you had to go back and change some of the work already completed. Many times agreed-upon strategies must change due to unforeseen information. Although that's entirely understandable, unnecessary delays in communicating these changes to those most affected by them are a symptom of this malady.

A second form of this affliction occurs when ineffective communication creates a crisis situation for those working with the supervisor. You may have thought to yourself, "If I'd only had the information that was decided days ago, I wouldn't be in this last-minute rush, coming in early to complete the task!" Again, some of this fallout is unavoidable from time to time. In this case, however, we're discussing a habit, not an occasional lapse. Why should a lack of planning on the part of your supervisor have to constitute an emergency for you?

Another form is a supervisor's failure to express appreciation in a manner that's effective for those working with that supervisor. In this instance, the boss usually expresses thank-yous in the manner that he or she likes best—not in the manner most effective for those working with him or her. My personal preference for being appreciated means having the trust and freedom to do my tasks without too much interference from supervisors. You may prefer more recognition and a verbal thank-you. One form isn't better than the other; they're just different.

2. Chronically disorganized and last minute, and prefers to make everything a crisis

This symptom refers to those supervisors who can't seem to keep focused on what's most important at that point in time. Or they're habitually late in completing their tasks before passing them on to you—with the hope that you can then work miracles in a very short time. This malady exists if you frequently find yourself thinking, "If only my supervisor could plan his [or her] work a little better . . ."

Some supervisors work best under pressure and assume that others do too. Others may be addicted to or simply enjoy the adrenaline push that occurs when facing down a deadline. Never able to move past the late-night cramming for college projects and exams, these supervisors still operate in a last-minute rush. The result? Those serving with these types of supervisors can be observed hastily trying to fulfill their duties with too little time before a deadline.

3. Unpredictable and frequently changing their minds without warning

Some jokingly remark that the only thing predictable about these types of supervisors is that they will be unpredictable. They're nearly always unable, unwilling, or uncertain about making a decision—and sticking with that decision. Staff members are left wondering if a decision has been made in the first place and what will be changed. Then they find themselves waiting until the last minute to begin a project because of those inevitable changes—changes that could happen up to the deadline.

4. Doesn't seem to understand another person's workload or how much time and effort it takes to complete a project

Usually this type of supervisor will ask questions like, "Why can't you (or they) get this done by then?" Or they'll say, "If they aren't able to do the job and get it done on time, then maybe I should just do it myself!" Both highlight another symptom of this disease: the inability to correctly pace work or the rate of change a team or an organization can manage. While everyone is working diligently on one change initiative, this supervisor is actively imagining yet another major change that the organization must tackle. The people around this kind of supervisor can't design and implement the systems required to execute the current change before another new, massive venture is enthusiastically announced by the supervisor.

I sometimes struggle with a form of this malady. As an optimistic, overactive change agent, I always believe that my team and I can always do . . . *more*. Are we truly able to leap tall mountains (we're in Colorado, you realize!) with a single bound? Not really, but some days a few of the staff here at the seminary may wonder about my ability to pace our rate of change! Recently one of the vice presidents even suggested that I take a one-year moratorium from introducing any change that wasn't absolutely necessary for the health of the seminary. It was hard for me to accept the advice, but he was definitely right in his observations. Therefore, this past year I've held myself in check, introducing a minuscule amount (from my perspective) of new initiatives. Only three pages worth.

5. Too much or too little of an open door policy

I try to maintain a balanced open door policy, one that offers sufficient access without allowing everyone else to dictate how my time and energies will be spent. It's a tenuous tightrope walk, for supervisors can fail in this area when they're over- *or* under-accessible. For example, they have massive lists of critical tasks, all demanding to be completed as soon as possible. But if they allow themselves to be ruled by these demands, they'll retreat to their offices—losing touch with the real needs, priorities, and challenges of the organization and staff.

The opposite swing of the pendulum can also be disastrous: allowing others to completely determine how you will invest your day, under the guise of being "always available," can cause equal damage to the organization. Finding the correct balance is difficult and crucial to the health of the organization.

6. Failure to effectively delegate and trust others, resulting in micromanagement

I've already discussed this more thoroughly in previous chapters, but let me try to describe this symptom as succinctly as possible: Insecurity, fear of failure, and desire for control are usually the motivators behind this expression of the affliction. These supervisors struggle to trust others and to believe that it's in the best interests of the organization for them to mobilize others to effectively complete their responsibilities.

7. Virtually ignores leading the department where you serve and spends all of his or her time leading another department

This lack of attention may result from having too much leadership responsibility, enjoying one area of the organization over another, or being too focused on problem solving instead of being proactive and strategic. The supervisor may be thinking that so many problems exist in the other department, and yours is doing just fine, so you don't need as much of the supervisor's attention. This usually produces an organizational decline in both departments due to too much attention on problem solving.

Treatment

I've addressed this malady from the supervisor's vantage point elsewhere. In the first part of this treatment section, I'll focus on how you can help your supervisor by improving your skills. In the second part I'll focus on what to do when you have done all you can to help your supervisor and he will not or cannot improve.

How you can help your supervisor by improving your skills

First, attempt to better understand your supervisor. What are his work strengths and weaknesses? Are there some things you might do to help enhance these strengths and manage the weaknesses—without assuming too much responsibility? How does she like you to seek information or solicit feedback? What about initiative? Does your supervisor want you to anticipate and fix things *before* asking for feedback? Or does he prefer that you seek his feedback before making changes? Does your supervisor like input in a direct manner or in a softer and more indirect form? Does she prefer to work at the last minute? What are the traits and idiosyncrasies that you simply need to accept as part of the job? And what are other aspects that you might be able to improve in the working relationship?

Think about what levels of input and feedback your supervisor prefers. Does he prefer full details or only the critical, condensed form? Is your supervisor an internal or external processor? In other words, does she like to make decisions after privately reflecting or in the course of a conversation with you? What types of decisions does your supervisor like to make and what does he prefer that *you* make? What surprises your supervisor and requires that you give him advance warning or quick alerts? These are just a few of the questions you might reflect upon and, if appropriate, discuss with your supervisor. Understanding your supervisor allows you to adapt in order to improve your teamwork—which will eventually make your job easier.

Invest time proving your trust and loyalty. All supervisors need to know that those reporting to them will be loyal and trustworthy in all situations. A good way to build this trust is to begin by trusting your supervisor. Another strategy has to be making the decision to be utterly reliable. The supervisor needs to know that if you're given a task, she can completely trust your ability to get the project done in a timely and effective fashion. Try to never make your supervisor look bad or point out her weaknesses. It's never appropriate to initiate a conversation with others about how his inabilities in any areas create more work or a hassle for you. Joining gripe sessions with fellow employees usually produces no positive results and destroys trust between you and your supervisor.

Keep confidences at all times. When a final decision is made, it's then your role and responsibility to positively support that decision—even if you didn't agree. Never tell others that you wanted to do it a different way "but my boss made me do it this way" or anything similar to that. *Make a commitment* to publicly support your supervisor as much as possible. Privately expressing your lack of support to the supervisor provides an increased possibility that the supervisor will listen and make any needed changes.

Ask your supervisor to help you prioritize the tasks she has assigned to you. As a supervisor, I clearly operate like the mulch truck driver that comes to my house bi-annually; he drops a full load of mulch on the corner of my driveway for me to spread among the landscaping. I always feel overwhelmed looking at that mountain of mulch, but I know that mulch has to be delivered this way.

In the same way, when I'm assigning tasks to others, I tend to drop a load of stuff that seems insurmountable. Helping those around me to organize and prioritize these tasks—without micromanaging—helps everyone to get the job done without burning out. If your supervisor is like me, then ask him to help you break the long list into more manageable, prioritized pieces.

Ask your supervisor for a regularly scheduled meeting. Then come prepared and ready to make the most of that time. While I enjoy chatting and learning personal stories about staff, I'm rarely in the mood to simply brainstorm with someone about how to do the assigned work. When staff members come to me, I want them to already be organized, prioritized, and ready to maximize our time together.

These regularly scheduled meetings are a good way to deal with a supervisor who neglects your area. Come to these meetings prepared to get the information and decisions that you need to operate your area effectively. Make a list of topics you need to discuss, and email the list to the supervisor before you meet. When meeting, ask permission from the supervisor to work down your list. Usually I would say it something like this: "I know that you have a number of things on your agenda for our meeting. Would you like me to go first with my agenda items that I sent you, or do you prefer to work on your list first?"

Another strategy to use in these meetings is to ask questions about decisions or other forms of information that might assist you. Ask the supervisor if—after having more time to reflect on your last conversation—any of her thinking has changed or any decisions affecting your project have been revised since you last met. Do this in a matter-of-fact communication style, not in an argumentative or accusatory way. The key is to communicate that you are seeking additional feedback, not criticizing her.

Bring solutions—not just problems. A common mistake staff members make is to hope that supervisors will take over their challenges or make decisions for them. Wrong assumption! A word of caution here: some supervisors indeed may desire this role or can easily slip into micromanaging if given the chance. But don't give in to this illness. If you bring only problems, then the supervisor may take over and start to believe that *you aren't necessary*. Instead, try this approach: Clearly define the problem; explain the various risks involved in solving the problem; share the top two or three best solutions that you've carefully thought through; and then lastly, seek your supervisor's input. Ask good clarification questions after your supervisor offers feedback, including queries like "I think I'm hearing you say _____. Is that what you mean, or am I not fully understanding?" Other questions include, "If I start implementing that solution and discover (some problem), can I seek more of your feedback at that time?" Finally, try this: "What if I discover that this solution is producing different results than we anticipated, things like _____? Then I wonder if I could _____?"

Remember that the purpose is to show the supervisor that you can be trusted, you desire her feedback, and you will continue to assume wise leadership of the challenge. Nothing encourages me more than to know that I can trust a staff member to assume adequate responsibility for, seek appropriate feedback during, and actually lead a project. If this person repeatedly asks me to assume his or her responsibilities or provide the solutions, then I start to believe that one of us isn't really necessary. Usually that doesn't mean me!

Ask your supervisor if he would like to delegate to you anything from his list of responsibilities. If you notice any specific tasks that fit this category, ask your supervisor to consider delegating that area. Suggest something like, "I wonder if you might like me to assist you by _____?" Again, be careful here. Don't give the appearance or impression that you think your supervisor *needs* your help; rather, you're offering help by assuming responsibilities for tasks that a supervisor may appreciate having taken off her "to-do" list.

What to do if your supervisor can't improve

Define, understand, and accept your limitations. When you have done your part well and your supervisor fails to successfully complete his job, remember that you are not responsible for the supervisor's part. Yes, his failure may make you look unprofessional or incapable, but you can't control that. Trust God to be your defender and continue to accomplish your tasks well. You can't force your supervisor to take responsibility.

Allow your supervisor to feel the consequences of her failures. Yes, at times she may blame you for her failures, and that is so unfair and hurtful. Document all your efforts for future reference. Don't overprotect your supervisor. This only reinforces the poor behavior. Do your part to honor and glorify God, and trust that he will guide and reward you.

Confront your supervisor rarely and with extreme caution. No supervisor likes to be confronted on a regular basis, especially with an angry spirit. Select your time strategically. Try to pick a time that works best for the supervisor. Being confronted during a highly stressful time for the organization or when I'm tired from a full day of activities simply doesn't work for me. On some occasions choosing the time is out of your control, but attempt to do your best.

Also select a time for confrontation when you'll have control of your emotions. Angry, embittered, tear-filled confrontations lessen my ability to listen and make personal changes. Before proceeding, take time to reflect and organize your thoughts. Never confront on the spot or without time to prepare. And always try to confront before a situation becomes too major. A friend of mine tends to let things build up until he explodes with anger, and those on the receiving end rarely have any indication that things are going that badly.

As preparation for the confrontation with your supervisor, document as much as possible. Make a list of specific examples of the times and actions when your supervisor did not properly assist you in your role in the department. Most supervisors will not positively receive criticism from direct reports concerning their overall roles as a leader. Stick to how the supervisor can better help you, and if asked, then suggest ways he or she could improve as an overall leader. After the meeting, document the conversation and any agreed-upon courses of action. While it isn't your role to hold your supervisor accountable, having good documentation will help if future confrontations occur.

When actually confronting your supervisor, start by affirming what is going well and why you enjoy serving with her. Explain your motives for confronting; these will hopefully include the desire to more effectively serve your supervisor, better accomplish your tasks, and help the organization successfully complete its mission. Clearly define the problem as you see it, giving one or two objective examples of how the problem expresses itself. Then allow time for your supervisor to respond. Listen well and try not to become defensive or get into an argument with your supervisor. If the supervisor disagrees with your assessments and concerns, then try to clearly restate why you think and feel the way you do. When appropriate, move to positive suggestions for how the two of you could work together to overcome these challenges. Focus on your commitment to support the supervisor in making the changes.

Finish by talking about why you think these changes are important, and then conclude with another positive statement about the strengths of your supervisor. If your supervisor is an internal processor (you've obviously already noticed this beforehand), express that you know she may want some time to reflect before offering feedback. Add that you hope the two of you might have a follow-up conversation when she is ready.

If your supervisor is an external processor, then sit back and listen carefully, seeking to fully understand. Ask good clarification questions and be prepared not to defend yourself but to further explain, using specific examples of the problem and more positively stated solutions that might be considered. After listening to your supervisor's feedback, you may wish to ask for time to reflect. Suggest a follow-up conversation when you're ready for that to occur. Before the confrontation ends, reassure the supervisor of your support and the strengths that you appreciate. Your goal is to express your concerns within an environment of support and appreciation.

If you can adjust the way you work to better coordinate with your supervisor—and at the same time not feel compromised or resentful—then elect not to confront. Make the necessary adjustments. I know this sounds unfair, but it is the harsh reality of a peaceful and effective working relationship.

When is it appropriate to go to your supervisor's boss or solicit assistance from others? This is an extremely difficult question because the answer has to be based on actual elements within your specific context. Does your organization have an employee manual that explains how appeals should be handled? If the situation is hostile and you fear retaliation or punishment, how does your organization address these types of situations? If policies and procedures exist, carefully follow them and document all your actions.

Most Christian organizations will overtly affirm that when offenses occur between staff members, they should follow the biblical patterns of Matthew 18:15–17. Rarely do they actually follow the pattern, though. Regardless, I believe that as much as is possible within our power, we should attempt to follow these biblical guidelines. So generally only appeal to your supervisor's boss after you have tried to resolve the manner privately with your supervisor and when it is serious enough to warrant an appeal, it is a reoccurring problem, and you have documented clear evidence that supports your claims. If others are willing to participate in the appeal, you will find strength in numbers, but wait for those people to come to you with their concerns instead of recruiting others to join your cause. Pray that God might send these people to you. Ensure that these supporters will not withdraw, leaving you alone to face the consequences if things go poorly. Also be sure to allow enough prayer and time for God to work before appealing. Think in terms of weeks, not days, for God to work, unless the situation is so serious that the organization or people within the organization can or are being injured.

I have intentionally omitted immoral and illegal issues from this chapter. Consult your organization's policy manuals for how to deal with these issues. I am not an attorney and can't give you legal advice. From a biblical perspective, the principles of Matthew 18 still usually apply. However, I have seen far too many situations where staff members confronted a supervisor for moral or legal failure and lost their jobs or had their personal reputations severely damaged. In these situations, prayer and confidential wise counsel from trusted others are critical. Usually it is unwise to confront alone and better to have another person involved. Also, make sure you have indisputable proof—not rumors or hunches. It may be wise to only confront when you are an actual eyewitness to the event or when the actual person injured by the actions of the supervisor will be included. Document everything, and meet with the supervisor's boss immediately following your time with your supervisor, regardless of how your meeting with your supervisor went. I know these ideas sound contrary to the principles of Matthew 18, but you are in a precarious situation, and it is ultimately the boss's responsibility to deal with these concerns, not yours. Also, since you have not been personally offended, going to the supervisor's boss immediately with these types of serious situations probably does not violate the biblical principles. Once you have appealed, accept the decision or move on. Do not stay and continue to fight against the leadership of the organization where you serve. Trust God to provide a new place of service. Leave well.

A Final Word

Supporting and encouraging your supervisor will return multiple positive results. You'll encourage your supervisor to complete his or her tasks in a manner that ultimately assists *you*. Many times when supervisors feel supported, they become more open to positive suggestions for how they might improve the way they do their work. Remember that supervisors will trust and respect you to the level they believe that *you trust and respect them*. Always be loyal and keep confidences, and know your supervisor well enough to understand how best to approach him or her when the time arises. Above all, remember that prayer is your first and best strategy when needing to confront anyone. Be the best team member you possibly can be, and that will have an amazing impact on those with whom you serve.

15

General Diagnosis, Treatment, and Prevention

Principles to Consider

The following is a list of principles that I prayerfully consider when designing treatments for staff infections. I've applied these principles in specific situations throughout this book, but this chapter provides more of a checklist approach for your personal use. Please remember to *prayerfully* consider how or whether these principles should be applied in your ministry context and with the specific situation you are facing. Humbly seek wisdom from God.

1. Apply the golden rule: treat staff the way you wish to be treated.

Ask yourself these questions: How would I want to be treated by my supervisors or fellow staff members if I were suffering from a staff infection? In what ways would I want them to approach me and in what setting? As I reflect on this principle, I ponder and pray about these important questions. I do know that I would always want to be treated with confidentiality, respect, love, and the belief that I can and will improve.

2. Personally model the values, behaviors, and attitudes that you want the staff to uphold.

Staff members watch their fellow staff members and leaders, searching for consistency between what they say and what they do before they're willing to commit to change. When you ask others to commit themselves to a set of behaviors, values, and attitudes, nothing motivates them more than to observe *you* dependably living these challenges. For example, if you ask staff members to serve others and yet don't demonstrate a regular commitment to serve others yourself, no amount of persuasion can overcome this inconsistency. Unless you model servanthood yourself, you'll never persuade other staff to adopt this value.

3. Always act with full integrity, especially when it requires a personal price.

When dealing with staff infections, the person confronting normally has to pay a personal price. This may include time, energy, resources, sleepless nights, and sometimes attacks on your personal character. When we are assaulted, it's so hard not to retaliate or try to prove that the way you're dealing with this is honorable. Sometimes you may even feel justified in leaking just a portion of the confidential facts. *Don't do it!* I try to remember that God is my defender and ensure that my supervisor has all the information she needs to provide support. Remember this guideline: Honesty is the best policy; full disclosure usually is not.

Speaking truth in love is generally your best choice, but explaining too much detail can be dangerous and in many cases just isn't necessary. This is especially true when having to speak with the press and in other public venues about certain staff problems. Your role is to be up front and honest with those who need information, while at the same time protecting the innocent victims and the organization where you serve. This is a tough line to walk.

4. Be as confidential as possible while never promising total confidentiality.

In many situations we may have confidential information that we cannot and should not share. When the situation becomes intense and your integrity is being attacked, it may be tempting to reveal this to someone else. Fight that urge. Maintain that confidentiality and try to protect those affected as much as is within your power.

Try never to promise confidentiality beyond appropriate limits. When people ask me to keep something confidential, I try to respond in this manner: "I can't promise complete confidentiality, but you can trust me to appropriately handle any information you share." If people pressure me to share information that shouldn't be shared, I then say, "In order to protect the privacy of those involved in this situation, I can't share that information." This doesn't always work, but it does signal that you are *protecting* versus *covering up.*

5. Build solid and healthy relationships with staff before problems arise.

Treating staff infections is always more effective when you have previously created an atmosphere of trust and ongoing relationships with the staff you supervise or serve with. This doesn't require that you be best friends. It does mean that they have had ample opportunities to observe your trustworthiness and to experience your love and respect for them. If staff members believe that you are working for their best interests, to empower them for reaching their full potential in God's kingdom, they will more readily listen and accept your feedback in difficult situations.

6. Work to develop a caring, trustworthy, open, and approachable atmosphere.

Staff members want to be respected, to be trusted, and to know that the organization cares for them and their families. Being easily approachable is another key component. Inviting people to talk with you and communicating that you will appropriately alter your daily tasks in order to be available to them is important. Ask the staff to respond confidentially to this question: What organizational policies, practices, procedures, or other things that we do suggest that the senior leaders do not trust you as staff members? If you ask this question, then you also must be prepared to make the changes.

7. Confusion can and will occur, so repeated, careful conversations are necessary.

Human relationships and conversations are prone to confusion and misunderstanding—especially when conflict is involved. A practice that I use when confronting staff is to say, "Now that we are done with this meeting, a need to ask clarifying questions or to share other information may arise later. Please come see me, call, or email so that any misunderstandings are not allowed to intensify. Also, if you think you were misunderstood, you misunderstood my remarks, or you simply need to talk, let's get together ASAP."

Location is also critical to the conversation. If it is a quick conversation on a nonthreatening level or if it is a very serious and potentially conflict-filled conversation, then choose either your office or the office of your supervisor. Conversations that fall in between these two levels might be better received in a neutral, quiet setting away from the office.

8. Document everything.

Keep accurate and thorough records. Carefully document the clear, objective behavioral problems and the staff member's failure to correct these problems. Record all meeting dates, coaching attempts, and action steps. Outline the general purpose of each meeting, list who attended, and then summarize the discussion. Later ask the other person to respond in writing or through an email to your summary. If a third party was used, ask that person to also review and sign meeting summaries. Stay away from subjective impressions or attempts to explain motives for behavior. Stick to the facts.

If you are confronting your supervisor, see chapter 14 for detailed guidelines. Also remember to document everything as explained above. A key difference is that you should not ask your supervisor to sign your summary of the meetings. You can keep your personal records and still send a copy of your meeting summary to the supervisor asking if he or she agrees with your assessment of your conversation. Keep or document any responses your supervisor offers to your summary of the meeting.

9. Sometimes—but not always—a wise, trusted, objective third party should be involved in the process to protect all parties and assist in effective communication.

A third party's observations can prevent a lot of misunderstandings and possible accusations. And even if they don't prevent misunderstandings, having a third party involved can protect you. Having someone with whom to discuss the meeting and process the next steps can also be extremely helpful. Remember to choose a wise and trustworthy person who is acceptable to both parties. Generally, you should alert the person you are confronting to the fact that another person will be joining the meeting. Surprising the staff member with a third party when he or she comes to the meeting is not a wise idea. I usually do not involve a third party the first time I discuss problems with staff members. More often I include a third party after previous attempts to help have failed. When alerting a staff member that a third party will join our meetings, I usually say something like, "I have invited (name the third party) to join us for our next meeting concerning (name the problems you will address). Do you trust him or her to be an objective third party to our discussion, or would you prefer someone else?" If they agree, then I proceed. If they disagree, then I try to negotiate with them on a mutually agreeable person.

Using a third party to participate in the conversation may signal that the conversation is quite formal and serious. If you desire a more low-key type of conversation and judge that the two of you can reach an acceptable solution, do not involve a third party.

10. Listen to understand, and restate what you're hearing to demonstrate that you do understand— even if you disagree.

Your goal is not to merely listen to words; it's to understand the *person*. You'll probably need to sort through some defensiveness and justifications, but you should listen carefully to learn all the facts and nuances of the problem—not to argue for your viewpoints. Try to remember that you aren't there to prove something or demonstrate that your viewpoint is correct. You *are* there to love that staff member and point him or her to a path of health. Restate to the person what you think you are hearing, remembering to stay on point. Don't fall into the trap of allowing the person to deflect the conversations to other ancillary issues.

11. Always keep your supervisor or a trusted elder or board member in the loop, seeking his or her support and advice whenever possible.

Don't attempt to deal with staff infections without the support of your supervisor. Additionally, before you confront a staff member, schedule a time to debrief your supervisor immediately following your confrontation meeting. This is critical. Nothing disarms an "end run" faster than the confronted staff member showing up at your supervisor's office to request a meeting—and finding you already there, waiting for your scheduled appointment.

12. Keep the staff member responsible for solving his or her problems; never assume more responsibility than you should.

Long-lasting and comprehensive healing usually results when those suffering from the illness take personal responsibility for their treatment. When you confront staff members, they may try to sabotage your efforts and deny their need to improve by shifting responsibility for their healing to you. Fight this tendency. If you are intervening in an infection that involves a squabble between multiple staff members, remember that the two offending staff members may either (1) attempt to make you the cause of their interpersonal problems, or (2) subtly try to give you the responsibility for solving the problems. Again, keep the responsibility with the staff members.

13. Do not reassume tasks that were delegated to others unless complete failure is about to occur.

Instead of reassuming responsibility delegated to an individual or group, work to redirect their efforts without discouraging them—unless the health of the institution is at stake or the team is falling into disarray. Diagnose what went wrong by asking yourself these questions: Did I poorly communicate my instructions, or were they misunderstood? Did the team leader not perform well? Did I assemble the wrong team members? Is team conflict the problem? Was the challenge too great, was the deadline unrealistic, or were not enough resources given to the team to help them succeed?

After understanding the causes for failure, plan your course of action. Sometimes you need to replace the team leader (do this carefully), or you may need to meet once with the team to brainstorm ways to return the team to productive work (use this method sparingly). Try to keep the focus on the team leader and allow the leader to facilitate the brainstorming process while you participate—not lead. If the issue is that you do not support their conclusions and recommendations, then appropriately thank and disband the team. Delay any additional initiatives in that area for a protracted period of time, then reconstitute a new team to explore other options. Remember that the best approach is to preclude these problems from occurring by carefully selecting the team leader, honestly sharing expectations and feedback guidelines, and providing necessary resources.

14. Because most staff infections involve both emotional and logical facets, treatment will require about 70 percent emotional and 30 percent logical work.

Carolyn is emotionally empathic and well balanced; with time and process she can also approach things with good, logical reasoning. I am logical and analytical; I'm also a bit emotionally underdeveloped, but with time and process, I can also work through the emotional side of issues. Therefore, I must regularly remind myself that in staff infection situations, logical answers and solutions usually do not win the day. As a matter of fact, they may actually limit your effectiveness. To counteract this tendency (which you may also have), I try to process the emotional side of a conversation ahead of time with Carolyn and some other person whom I trust. Making high demands on the confronted person to quickly move to logical solutions can be detrimental to the restoration process. A better approach might be to give him or her time to emotionally process as needed.

15. When a problem arises with a specific staff member, address it personally with that staff member alone.

If you have a problem with one staff member, do not use the poor leadership tactic of veiling or softening your response through new all-staff policies or general announcements that only demoralize your effective staff. A few years ago I heard that a Christian organization was having difficulty with its general receptionist. (This was before the current use of computers to handle incoming calls.) Instead of working with the receptionist individually and pointing out his inadequacies, the entire staff was required to attend a half-day training session on "how to answer phone calls." Needless to say, the staff was perplexed and angry with this poor decision by the leadership. Making blanket announcements or policies in an effort to fix an individual staff problem demoralizes and confuses the staff members who are performing their duties well. Be courageous and wise. Treat individual problems individually and group problems on a group level.

16. Be prepared to be attacked for being the messenger.

None of us enjoys being confronted about our behavior. Reflect for a moment on the last time your spouse, parents, siblings, or close friend confronted you. Did you eagerly respond with great enthusiasm and wonderful strategies for improvement? Reflect for another moment or two and then respond *truthfully*! Unfortunately, in some staff situations, the staff member being confronted will attack you, the process you followed in confronting, or even others—all in an effort to keep from facing their issues. Be prepared for this, as noted in numerous chapters in this book. Remember, your job is to stay calm and keep redirecting the conversation back to the issue at hand. Do not allow them to take the offensive. Keep bringing them back by saying, "We will discuss those concerns at another time. Right now we are here to discuss (whatever the behavioral/performance problem is)."

17. Be intentional about dealing with the personal stress this will create for you.

Handling conflict exacts a costly price physically, emotionally, and spiritually. To deal with this stress you'll need to pray, keep a journal, practice the other spiritual disciplines, talk regularly with a friend, exercise, and/or enjoy a hobby. Trying harder or being more committed isn't the answer—living a healthy life on all these levels is. I gave up trying to live a "balanced life" a long time ago. Instead, I want to live a *healthy* life based on correct priorities and life principles. Therefore, I attempt to love God, my wife, and my family with all my heart, soul, and mind. I exercise regularly, try to eat healthy foods and enjoy some hobbies, and consistently practice Sabbath rest. No, Sabbath rest doesn't mean I take Saturday or Sundays off! I used to be a pastor serving in a congregation which had multiple services over both Saturday and Sunday, and now as president of a seminary, many weekends are filled with activities for the school—obviously negating the possibility of total rest on either day. Sabbath rest means that I do regularly set aside and take time to rest, reflect, worship, and refresh. I have found that during the actual time of a staff member crisis, I usually can't take as much time to rest as needed, but I try to get as much as I can. Following the time of conflict, I plan an extended time away to rest and refresh.

18. Healthy leaders do not relish or seek conflict but they appropriately embrace and lead through conflict.

No healthy (or sane!) person enjoys conflict. But leaders must embrace conflict and lead the best they can while relying on God to guide. Ignoring conflict actually allows it to intensify and potentially consume an organization. Putting off conflict can eventually require more time, effort, and resources than it would have if you had dealt with it at an earlier stage. If "peace at all costs" is your goal, you will never reach it.

Remember that some conflict is actually healthy. Resolving issues surrounding healthy conflict can clarify your organizational mission, vision, and values. If you lead effectively through the conflict, you may also find that you have earned a deeper level of respect and trust among the staff. Courage and faith are at the heart of leading change—for they bring forth wisdom and the power of the Spirit to accomplish even greater things.

19. Be proactive instead of reactive.

Directing a process instead of *reacting* to it is always a wiser and easier course. Staff members suffering from certain maladies will try to take you off track and back you into a defensive or reactive mode in an attempt to keep you from exposing their illness. Anticipating what steps a confronted staff member might take next and being ahead of him or her usually helps. Informing and seeking the support of a supervisor or other key staff member before you confront an ill staff member is one example of being proactive.

20. Carefully think through when a spouse should be involved in the conversation and as a partner in the solutions.

This a tough decision for you to consider. Having the spouse of the staff present can be threatening to the staff member and is inappropriate in most cases. However, at times this could be a wise and valid choice. I don't discuss moral issues and illnesses in this book because they are beyond my expertise, but I have dealt with this on a staff level. Treating an addiction to pornography or other forms of sexual immorality may be offenses that require the involvement of the staff member's spouse. But involving the spouse when you first meet with a staff member may not be the best choice. Sometimes a spouse has come to me with information on his or her spouse's illness. Don't allow yourself to be placed in the middle of the two spouses. When this does occur, I refer the couple to an outside trusted counselor who can provide the necessary guidance.

21. Think through the timing of intervention.

This principle is hard. The goal is to intervene at the most appropriate time—not too early nor too late. Our tendency is to wait too long to act—and push too far too quickly after finally deciding to act. If we've waited too long, the illness may be so consuming that treatment now requires major surgery. I wish I could give you clear and definitive advice on timing, but I can't. Remember that sometimes the staff members need to solve their problems without outside intervention. When the problems start negatively affecting other staff, the staff member's family, the organization, or you, it is probably time to intervene. Work hard to not allow your frustration level to build so high that when you finally confront the staff member, you surprise them with the full intensity of your pent-up frustrations. Reflect upon your track record. Do you tend to wait too long—or intervene too soon? How can you adjust your timing to mitigate this timing tendency?

22. If necessary, wait for God to provide more evidence, eye witnesses, answers, and resources—without using this as an excuse to not lead.

Sometimes information comes to you in an unconfirmed or suspect fashion. It could be that the person bringing the communication or the information itself doesn't seem quite right. At other times you may have suspicions about a staff member, or you may be hearing rumors. You also may find that when talking with a supervisor—seeking his or her support to confront a staff member—you aren't certain that the supervisor is on board. In these types of situations, wait on God to provide more witnesses, more trustworthy information, confirmation of previous accounts, your supervisor's support, and/or undeniable evidence. Remember, God has concerns about his honor and the honor of your organization. Wait and proceed only when truly ready, and never do so on a mere hunch.

23. Don't forget that sometimes problems will take care of themselves and you need not overreact; instead, just wait it out.

Sounds contradictory to the other principles, doesn't it? And yet, sometimes it *is* best to let a problem work itself out. If a staff member is suffering from a staff infection of some sort and it's not negatively affecting your organization or other members of staff, wait until God gives you a clear and open door to address this with the staff member—or simply let God control the situation as he wishes. Don't be overly aggressive in confronting.

24. When interacting with the press or other public figures, do not cover up or give the appearance of covering up.

If you must make public comments, heed this advice: Don't share confidential information. Don't say "no comment." If possible, prepare in advance with the help of a professional. Speak deliberately, but not too fast or too slow. Look the reporter or camera in the eye with appropriate emotion. Match your body language to the situation. Try to carefully share the mission and values of the institution. Be straightforward in your answers. Never give more information than requested. Acknowledge emotions and struggles while deflecting inappropriate questions by saying, "It's important that I protect the privacy of the individuals involved," or, "For the sake of those affected by all this, it is not appropriate for me to discuss that issue in a public venue." Also talk about what proactive steps you have taken to address the issue and about how the institution takes this problem seriously and is committed to resolving it.

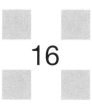

16

Establishing a Positive and Encouraging Bedside Manner

Building an Appreciative and Affirming Culture

What makes you feel most appreciated as a staff member?

- A pat on the back with a kind word
- A large salary increase
- Recognition in front of your peers or the public
- More vacation time
- More responsibility or freedom
- Larger program budget
- Bonus or gift certificate

- Feeling trusted and respected
- A desk of your own with business cards
- A combination of this list
- Other

Anyone who's ever been on a staff knows that people feel appreciated in different ways. As a leader, your challenge is matching the way you appreciate staff with the method that is most effective for an individual staff member. Personally, I feel the most appreciated when given the freedom, trust, and respect needed to effectively fulfill my responsibilities. I detest being micromanaged and find that both my motivation and ability to do a good job diminish when this occurs. When I'm micromanaged, it's clear to me that one of us is not necessary and that I'm not valued as a contributing staff member.

Yes, salary increases are important, especially if a staff member's compensation is significantly lower than that of his or her peers. However, numerous research studies have shown that salary increases actually have a limited ability to make staff members feel appreciated for an extended time. Instead, helping them to feel trusted, respected, and valued over a long period may be the most effective way to show that paid or unpaid staff members are appreciated.

In this chapter, we'll look at some practical strategies for building an organizational culture of appreciation and trust. Building this type of organization doesn't occur overnight; it frequently requires numerous training sessions for those who supervise. The goal is for paid and unpaid staff to feel consistently trusted and valued for their contributions to the mission of the organization where they serve. Successfully valuing others will produce increased retention, more productive staff, greater fulfillment of mission, and a more enjoyable experience for everyone. Though you most likely have a list of strategies of your own, compare the following with yours and then design a plan to build and sustain an organizational climate of trust and appreciation at your organization for the long haul.

Strategies for Building a Culture of Appreciation

1. Start by becoming a positive, affirming person who proactively helps other supervisors to do the same.

As always, we begin with the need to personally model the values and changes you wish to uphold or implement. Approaching life from a negative perspective and sharing that negative vantage point with others will destroy any attempts to help staff members feel appreciated.

For my Christmas present, Carolyn signed both of us up for Tai Chi classes—the exercise form of the martial arts. The regular instructor understood that learning Tai Chi was a bit intimidating to a group of aging baby boomers who no longer possessed the athletic abilities of their younger years. So she chose to motivate us by pointing out what we were doing well. From this platform of affirmation she then shared some practical steps to help us improve our form and motivate us to learn the next routine.

Carolyn quickly proved to be a natural. As for me, well . . . it was not a pretty sight. Imagine an overweight, fifty-something-year-old with greatly diminished flexibility trying to express himself in an art form that requires balance and grace. Sorry, I probably shouldn't have put that mental image in your head. Let's move on.

One week we had a guest instructor (also an expert in Tai Chi), and he chose to spend his time pointing out all the things we needed to do to improve, with very little affirmation. When we students gathered the next week at the beginning of class, we informally shared how unpleasant and ineffective the previous week's instructor had been. And therefore it was no surprise that we made a pointedly unanimous decision to ask the regular teacher to review the previous week's routines. We needed help to overcome our newly acquired and lingering hesitancy.

Where do you fall as a coach and supervisor? Do you approach needed change from a platform of affirmation—or do you have a tendency to skip that key part and point out the deficiencies?

2. Trust others and show this trust in the way you lead.

One of the most critical—if not *the* most important—roles of a leader is the ability to empower and trust others to do the work of the organization. This difficult task requires that you embrace these key factors: you must accept and make peace with the fact that you can't and shouldn't control or personally lead everything in the organization where you serve. Effective senior leaders realize that their success as leaders and the success of the organization depend upon their ability to let go. They need to trust others with some of the most important and risky aspects of the ministry.

Trusting in this manner means that senior leaders depend upon others for their overall success as leaders. This realization can lead to a personal insecurity that produces anxiety, resulting in micromanaging out of fear of failure. Yet not trusting others to fulfill their tasks damages the organization by decreasing the overall morale and effectiveness of the staff. It can be a vicious cycle. I'm not suggesting blind or foolish trust. I am suggesting a trust built over a period of time of serving together. Usually this "trust bank account" means that we initially grant trust with larger amounts of supervision and then over time grant more trust with less supervision.

Wise trust doesn't suggest that leaders abdicate their need to supervise. It suggests that "I can trust you to do your job well," and therefore, "You need to welcome and seek my input at appropriate stages and within agreed-upon guidelines." Trust given is trust received. It's matching appropriate levels of authority with equitable levels of responsibility. Remember that sometimes, in order to build trust as supervisors, we need to allow the other person to make decisions that are different from what we would make—but will still work.

This is especially true as we supervisors grow older and work with younger staff. They need room to try different ideas and experiment. Remember also, as explained in previous chapters, to never make decisions for staff members that they should make for themselves. Your role is to give insight and encouragement—not to make decisions for them.

3. Provide consistent support.

Providing sufficient levels of support for others to complete their responsibilities is vital to building a culture of appreciation and trust. This support includes having a listening ear and open door policy, lending your authority when needed, and allocating a sufficient amount of needed resources.

My schedule never seems to have enough time in it to complete all that needs to be done—not to mention all the traveling I do. Still, I try to practice an open door policy in which people feel free to approach me and don't need to wait unduly to interact with me. I do set times when I'm just not available. All leaders must manage their time well and reserve times for limited interruptions. I've discovered that I can expand my availability through email, cell phone, and training the staff closest to me to answer most routine questions so that people can receive information quickly. However, leaders still need to give ample opportunities for meeting face-to-face with others to provide a listening ear, encouragement, wise input, and corrective instructions. Others feel respected and valued when they know they can count on you to give as much time as possible to assist them.

At other times, staff members need us to lend our authority to help them accomplish their tasks. Helping them cut through bureaucracy, red tape, and passive or overtly aggressive resistance are just a few examples of when we might need to extend our authority to enable others to complete their tasks.

At a ministry where I was serving, I had requested that Jerry meet with other members of our staff on my behalf to ask them for support of a major change initiative that we were implementing. Jerry was to be the primary leader. To his and my surprise, during the meeting one young member of the staff stated that Jerry obviously didn't understand how busy he was; he said that he'd get to the requested tasks once he had finished other duties.

To Jerry's credit, he kept his emotional response under control and simply stated that he was there representing me, so this staff member should understand it was the *senior* leader's request—not merely Jerry's. Once again the young staff member stated that he would get to these tasks when he was ready to do so. As you can imagine, other members immediately began wondering if they also could delay implementing these challenging new tasks based on their personal priorities.

Later, when Jerry relayed the details of this encounter, we discussed how we should proceed. I sent out a "personal invitation" to this particular staff member, asking him to come to my office. There I privately explained that from this point forward, he was to show Jerry all the respect that he should show to me, or else he could find another place of service. He was deeply apologetic, and to his credit, he immediately assumed these new tasks, completing them successfully within the needed time frame and with no further complaining.

From that point on, whenever Jerry approached him, this young staff member was a model employee. And as the story quickly moved throughout the entire organization, Jerry now had the official endorsement he needed to complete his tasks. These stories don't always end well, but this story does illustrate how we need to leverage our authority for others.

Allocating sufficient resources for a person or team to successfully complete their responsibilities is another method for developing trust and appreciation. At times I have served on or assembled teams to accomplish significant assignments with scarce resources. When this occurs, I try to be honest about the limited means, making it clear that a major part of their assignment would be securing needed resources. Setting this exception aside, when you delegate work to a person or team, they need to know what resources are available, know when to come to you for additional needs, and believe that you have allocated sufficient resources for their success. And yes, my experience has generally been that everyone wants more funds as the first method to solve problems. Unfortunately, most organizations have very limited funds. You'll need to encourage your teams to use creative thinking rather than merely requesting more money as the first solution.

4. Spend time getting personally acquainted with staff members.

Before we hire paid or unpaid staff members, I always meet with the prospective staff member before the final decision is made. My purpose isn't to interfere with the hiring process—and I don't do it because I don't trust others to recruit their staff. Instead, I want the opportunity to connect personally with that potential staff member, hearing his or her heart and passions and searching for a connection with our institutional heart and passions. I also intend to explain our organizational mission, values, and vision; to immediately help that new staff member understand that he or she is becoming a significant part of our community; and to demonstrate that I value this new member enough to learn his or her name and some pertinent personal information. This has worked well over the years and has been greatly appreciated by our new staff members. Sharing this personal time and knowing their names allows me to greet them and ask about their family and previous jobs.

Another practice that I use periodically is to arrange all the staff into diverse small groups. I then invite these small groups to join me for lunch—my treat. "Brown bagging it" can work too. During this lunch I ask non-threatening personal questions about family and hobbies, giving each staff member an opportunity to talk before the whole group. Then I move to questions like, "If you had a magic wand and could change anything at our organization, what would it be?" Or, "If you had a magic wand and could ensure that one thing would never change, what would that be?" Another favorite question is, "What is the one thing you are currently working on that gives you the greatest joy or excitement?" These informal gatherings can take months to complete but have proven to be one of the most enjoyable and worthwhile things I've done. If you have a smaller number of staff, try meeting monthly as a whole group to enjoy lunch and a fun conversation together.

I also send cards to all our staff members for their birthdays and anniversaries. During our monthly staff meetings, I intentionally sit with staff members that I have limited contact with, and before the meeting begins, I try to engage them in fun conversations about their latest favorite movie or any hobbies I know they enjoy. This small talk goes a long way in providing an atmosphere of trust and respect.

5. Be predictable and give open and honest feedback.

My goal is that no staff members will ever hear information from the "rumor mill" that they haven't heard from me first. I'm not suggesting leaders violate confidentiality, and some information needs to be shared only at appropriate times and settings. But when staff members are left wondering—and worse yet, speculating—about what's happening, they become insecure, then quickly feel disrespected. While some leaders think it's wise to withhold information for the sake of power and control, openly sharing information actually releases power and control to the *entire* staff. This energizes the organization as a whole to fulfill its mission more effectively.

To further help with open communication, disseminating information, and quelling rumors, we include a session of what we call "put the president on the hot seat" at our monthly staff meetings. During this time staff members can ask any question they wish. My response must be open and straightforward, and I'm not allowed to put any "presidential spin" on the answer. Everyone understands that I won't share confidential information; they've also learned that I'll share all that I can. This isn't easy, but it's so important. I also spend some time telling personal stories about recent events in my life (especially ones concerning my grandchildren!). Sharing in this way has helped staff members to see me as more approachable; they're more likely to come talk with me one-on-one if they know they'll be greeted with a relaxed, warm atmosphere.

Being predictable is another key component in building a culture of trust and appreciation. I once consulted with a senior leader who was like a Chihuahua on a triple shot of espresso. The only predictable thing about him was his unpredictability! He changed either his mind or the direction of the institution so often that people never knew what decisions had been made. They also knew he could change a decision at any point if he thought of a new idea—regardless of whether it was a good one. Trust is destroyed by senior leaders in these types of organizations.

When people judge that their supervisor has their best interests in mind, they can receive and even welcome open and honest feedback on their performance as staff members. You may be wondering how you can communicate to others that you have their best interests in mind. First, start from a platform of repeated affirmation. Then offer your feedback with a commitment to help coach them, giving some solutions they can consider. Also, try to always correct in private—never in public. If it does become absolutely necessary to rebuke in public, try to meet one-on-one with the staff member to discuss further and explain why you had to use the public setting. Remember that for the majority of staff, *a whisper of criticism is a shout when it comes from the senior leader*. Speak well of all staff members when discussing a staff person with other staff. Be fair and consistent while handling the unique aspects of working with multiple staff.

6. Publicly and privately recognize accomplishments of staff.

Privately saying thanks and acknowledging accomplishments are important parts of helping others feel appreciated. However, nothing encourages staff more than to be recognized for their accomplishments in front of their peers. You may have a few staff members who are so shy that they say they don't want any public recognition, but my experience has been that they really don't mean it.

Saying that you appreciate someone or a team in front of others is far more effective if you connect that thanks to specific behaviors that you valued. During the time we relocated the seminary, I discovered that sharing a general thank-you to all the staff members for their hard work was not really that helpful. When I started saying thank you by pointing out specific accomplishments by individuals or teams, the smiles grew bigger and the nods larger. They needed to know that I understood not just that they had worked hard but that they had successfully overcome obstacles and challenges. That I could talk about those things with a level of specificity demonstrated that I truly understood.

One example that's still vivid in my mind is the team that worked diligently behind the scenes to strategically give away all the furniture that we weren't going to take with us to the new campus. When I told the story of how they had selected specific urban and under-funded ministries throughout the metro Denver area and then read thank-you letters from the ministry leaders who had received this furniture, the effectiveness of my saying thanks grew exponentially.

7. Design fun and inexpensive times of enjoyment into the life of your organization.

At our staff meetings we've occasionally planned times to brainstorm ideas of inexpensive and fun things we could do together to simply relax and enjoy each other's company. One of my favorite ideas was miniature golf day at one of the churches I served. On that day each department designed its own golf hole in the church, and the creativity was unbelievable! One of the best holes was designed in multiple steps; it eventually ended with the golf ball being putted through an enlarged picture of the mouth of the senior leader! Not quite so high on my list, however, was the golf hole that ended with the ball coming to rest in a toilet in the bathroom. Any guesses which department designed that one? If you've ever been on a church staff, you'll recognize immediately the unique creativity of the youth department.

Books and the Internet are sources for ideas of hundreds of innovative, fun, and inexpensive events to say thanks. You definitely don't need a lot of money to say thanks and have fun together.

8. When possible, budget funds to use to say thanks.

After the relocation of the seminary was completed, we took all the staff members who served on the numerous relocation task forces (with their spouses or a family member or friend) to a musical theatrical performance followed by dinner. It was a wonderful evening! This was a more costly thank-you, but we had allocated those funds into our overall relocation costs. One-day or overnight retreats (with or without spouses) can also be effective in demonstrating appreciation.

Occasionally, free dinners or free nights in a nice hotel with spouses are appropriate gifts to demonstrate appreciation for exemplary service. Gift cards to someone's favorite store can show people they are valued. By being creative, you can offer much-appreciated gifts even in the range of twenty-five dollars. Extra days off or increased vacation time are great thank-yous too. If you've ever wondered about overdoing a thank-you, follow the front page of the newspaper rule: if what you did to say thanks showed up on the front page of the local newspaper, would it withstand public scrutiny?

9. Implement a merit raise system for all compensation.

While I believe this idea is solidly biblical, what I'm about to suggest may not sound Christian or biblical to you. Obviously you'll need to decide this issue for yourself, but first carefully read and reflect on Matthew 25:14–30 before finalizing your thoughts. I believe this parable illustrates that the faithful and effective use of gifts deserves a greater reward, and that all will be held accountable for their efforts.

For all paid staff members, base their entire salary increase on the quality of their performance. You must explain in advance the criteria that will be used and apply this agreed-upon criteria fairly. Also, paid staff persons shouldn't be surprised when they're informed of any lowered level of compensation increases. As soon as problems arise, the paid staff member should be informed and given the opportunity to improve. Additionally, use a compensation committee (it may include board members at some levels) to assist you when making compensation decisions. *Never make those decisions alone.*

Several years ago Carolyn and I were attending a small dinner party with about forty financial friends of the organization where I served. During my presentation time, I thanked the donors for their gifts, noting that they made it possible for us to give year-end bonuses to our paid staff who hadn't received a salary increase in two years. When I returned to the table where I was sitting, a longtime employee asked me if these bonuses were going to be based on longevity of service—right in front of the donors at our table. Without thinking, I responded by saying, "No, the amounts will be based on how much you've flattered the senior leader!" It was bold and effective—causing a good deal of laughter at our table—but not a very wise comment. I recovered quickly and announced that the bonuses would be based on everyone's quality of service over the past year.

After the dinner a donor thanked me for my humor. She also affirmed that if I hadn't stated that the bonuses were to be given on a merit basis, she wouldn't have given another gift because she would judge that I wasn't wisely using the gift she'd already given.

Please don't misunderstand: I'm not suggesting that we give raises based on what donors think. I am trying to illustrate that supporters of your organization expect you to be a wise steward of the resources they've invested in your ministry; using merit increases is one wise approach. And though we do need to acknowledge long-term commitment and service by paid staff members, their continued effective service is even more critical.

A Final Word

Everyone loves and needs to be trusted, respected, and appropriately appreciated. With a modest amount of effort and resources, you can build an atmosphere within your organization where paid and unpaid staff members feel valued. When people sense that they are appreciated, they will perform at higher levels of effectiveness and be more internally motivated to serve. With intentional and consistent effort, you can accomplish this.

Finally, above all the ideas I've listed in this chapter is this one central act: pray regularly—by name—for each staff member. Prayer *is* our life in Christ. Your effectiveness in leading staff depends on a mind, heart, and soul transformed by prayer.

17

Working with Unpaid Staff

Similarities with and Differences from Paid Staff

Recently when I was teaching a group of pastors on leading staff, one of the pastors stated that we could never treat unpaid staff in the way I was suggesting. He condescendingly corrected me and shared with the rest of the class that he had only one paid staff member and a couple dozen unpaid staff; therefore, he knew what was best when leading unpaid staff. So, I had a choice to make: I could get into a contest with him and prove who was right, or I could ignore his attitude and try to answer his real question.

The unspoken question was, *What are the similarities and differences when leading unpaid staff versus paid staff?* There are definitely critical differences—and similarities. In this chapter I hope to provide a meaningful discussion of a list of principles that explain what I judge are the key elements when supervising unpaid staff. In the last two churches I served, we boldly stated in our publications that listed staff that every member of the church was called to be a minister of the gospel, and the paid staff were responsible for mobilizing each church member for effective service in God's kingdom. This helped to prevent any thinking among paid or unpaid staff that one class of staff was more spiritual or called by God while the other was not.

Similarities in Supervising Paid and Unpaid Staff

1. Both paid and unpaid staff desire to serve well.

Yes, there are exceptions to this principle, but the common belief that unpaid staff only want to assume minimal responsibilities and complete their duties at a mediocre level is false. Properly recruited and mobilized unpaid staff are just as motivated to serve well as paid staff—and at times are even more motivated.

In the organizations where I have served, I simply did not find the stereotypical unpaid staff member who was there to provide token service so they could "feel okay about serving God." Rather, I served with unpaid staff members who wanted to serve God with passion and in a manner that made a difference in the lives of others. When I came upon unmotivated or underperforming un-paid staff, it was usually because the paid staff members (including me) had not done an adequate job in helping the unpaid staff member succeed.

I know these are strong ideas and you may disagree. But if you do find that you have mostly unmotivated and underperforming staff, you probably need to take a step back; reflect on what message you're sending to the unpaid staff; and finally, scrutinize the way you're recruiting and mobilizing them for ministry. Are you inadvertently telling those you're recruiting that the role doesn't require commitment? It's tough to say and to receive this strong message, but *you* may actually be the problem, not your unpaid staff—especially if you are in some subconscious way communicating to them that you don't trust or value them.

2. Both paid and unpaid staff want a clear sense of the tasks you're asking them to complete.

When recruiting unpaid staff members, you need to always provide a clear ministry description. Don't use the phrase "job description," because that creates some legal implications that you don't want to imply. Instead, in your ministry description explain the basic responsibilities, reporting structure, desired outcomes, review process, and general time commitment—*honestly*. Also include a clear sense of what you'll expect of them and what they can expect from you as their supervisor. Explain in person why this position is important to the institution and why you're specifically asking them to prayerfully consider serving in this capacity. Define what resources are available to the unpaid staff member and also any basic procedures, rules, or values that need to be followed. Spending approvals, budget guidelines, use of credit cards, and reimbursement for mileage are a few examples. Treat your interview and recruiting efforts seriously.

3. Both paid and unpaid staff members will do a better job if they know their efforts are appreciated.

Although sometimes we forget to thank paid staff because they're compensated for their work, probably more frequently we forget to intentionally appreciate the unpaid staff. It doesn't require a lot of effort to say thanks to these dedicated people who serve out of commitment and passion for God and your institution. In the previous chapter I offered numerous examples for building an overall culture of trust and appreciation in your institution, and for unpaid staff, little things go a long way.

Business cards that list the name and contact information for your organization and the title of the unpaid staff member are one small way to say "you're important to us." Providing a small amount of office space where they can do their work may not be always necessary but can be a visible sign that you value their work. Thank-you notes or emails are always appropriate, and personal thanks and recognition in front of the rest of the paid and unpaid staff will also communicate appreciation. Remembering their names and in what areas they serve is good, but following up on that by asking specific questions about their ministry responsibilities and how things are going is even better.

4. Both paid and unpaid staff members value open communication.

It's incredibly frustrating to be the last to hear important information—especially when it relates to your area of service. Involving unpaid staff members in decisions that will affect their ministries sends a loud and clear message that they are valued at your institution. Seeking their counsel and feedback speaks volumes. Again, follow the rule that no unpaid staff member should hear important information from the rumor mill before they hear that information from you or their supervisors. Or, to state it differently, unpaid staff members should have all the pertinent information they need to do their jobs well. Hold regularly scheduled staff meetings that are required for all paid *and* unpaid staff. Be sure to explain this expectation to the unpaid staff members when they are first recruited.

5. Both paid and unpaid staff members need to be trusted to do their work well.

Here is where some of you may have strong reservations. If you have recruited a qualified unpaid staff member, he or she can be trusted to the *same level* as a paid staff member. Certainly few unpaid staff members can give equal amounts of time as paid staff. However, at most of the previous institutions where I've served, we always had at least one unpaid staff member who earned one dollar a year. This person was always a gifted early retiree, now financially wealthy and moving to a place where he or she could serve in an area of specific passion—desiring to make a difference. These "paid" staff members were invaluable to the organization, and most of them worked thirty or more hours per week.

In my opinion, when unpaid staff members aren't reaching the desired outcomes, it's usually because we didn't match the right person to the right ministry area; we didn't provide enough resources and adequate supervision; or we didn't do an adequate job in explaining why their positions were critical to the organization. Certainly some unpaid staff members don't work out. However, underperforming staff should motivate us to step back and reflect on what went wrong instead of assuming that unpaid staff members aren't trustworthy. Nothing could be further from the truth.

6. Both paid and unpaid staff need a regular and clear review process.

I regularly receive disparaging remarks when I offer this principle to pastors. Usually I hear, "Oh, you just

can't review unpaid staff members like you do paid staff."
Not true! You can indeed do so, and if they know when
recruited that they'll be reviewed at a later date, they will
actually welcome the process. Regular reviews communicate that both the person and position are important
to your organization and that you expect them to be
faithful in fulfilling their duties. Why would you or I sign
up to serve as an unpaid staff member if no one took
the job seriously enough to determine if it was being
accomplished?

For most unpaid staff members, a review ninety days
after first assuming the position and then an annual
review is sufficient. When reviewing unpaid staff members, ask them to complete self-reviews of their performances and then use these reviews as the basis for your
conversations. In the review discuss what's going well,
how much you've appreciated them, areas for improvement, and what you can do as their supervisor to help
them succeed.

Some senior leaders object at this point and argue
that if the supervisor were to suggest areas for improvement, the unpaid staff member might become
offended, resign, and leave the church or organization.
This viewpoint may be right in some cases—when
given honest feedback, some unpaid staff may resign
and leave. I wonder, however, what value underperforming, unpaid staff members are to the church or
organization when they're allowed (perhaps even encouraged) to keep serving out of fear that they might
leave? What is the real danger if poorly committed
people leave our churches or organizations? Would
the word get out that unless you're serious about your
commitment to serve, you shouldn't apply for unpaid
positions within that ministry? Is that too provoca-
tive? Or is it actually the type of committed service
that God asks of us all?

7. Both paid and unpaid staff members should be encouraged to recruit and mobilize other unpaid staff members.

If mobilizing unpaid staff to serve in your organization is a critical value, then both paid *and* unpaid staff members should be expected to focus on this recruiting task. While this may not always be true for all unpaid positions, it should generally be true. Who could be better suited to recruit others than unpaid staff members asking their qualified friends to join them in ministry? Make this a stated part of the ministry description and explain this expectation early in the recruiting process.

8. Churches and other institutions should do thorough background checks and ask for references for both paid and unpaid staff.

What a sad time in human history when we have to work so diligently to protect children, youth, the elderly, and our organizations from dangerous predators who roam around in search of places where they can devour innocent victims. As more and more secular nonprofit organizations tighten their background checks of potential paid and unpaid staff, these predators will turn more frequently to religious organizations that are lagging behind, not yet doing thorough background checks.

Sadly, due to threats of lawsuits, many organizations are afraid to share the sordid backgrounds of former paid or unpaid staff members, hoping that these problem staff members will just go away. More likely, they'll go to yet *another* ministry, seeking ever more victims. Open and fully disclosing references can be difficult to find. But we still must do our best to carefully learn all we can about any persons we're considering for either paid or unpaid positions. I am not an attorney, so please consult your church attorney for legal advice on how to give references on former staff. Many attorneys may encourage you to limit your references of former staff members to the dates of their employment, their titles and basic responsibilities, and whether they left in good standing with the organization. So you decide how best to handle these situations after consulting the attorneys and prayerfully seeking God for advice. Always complete criminal checks on any paid or unpaid staff who will work with children or youth.

Differences in Supervising Paid or Unpaid Staff

1. Unpaid staff members should have specific time limits on their service.

Unlike paid staff, unpaid staff members should be recruited for a one-year term, renewable subject to the annual review. The idea here is to provide an automatic system for the unpaid staff member or the supervisor to end the arrangement. If both of you know that the year has not gone well, everyone can save face by simply not renewing for another year. This one-year time span helps provide stability in the position for that year while not requiring unpaid staff members to sign up "for life"; it also provides relief from guilty feelings for not serving beyond one year. Interests and personal arrangements in the lives of unpaid staff members change, so having this regular possible end date helps everyone. Make this expectation clear when first recruiting and include it in the ministry description.

2. When unpaid staff members are terminated, they may or may not leave the church.

This may sound confusing. When paid staff are terminated, it's rare that they wouldn't go to another place of employment. Terminated unpaid staff members, however, have more choices. They may stay and cause conflict within the church, they may stay and be happily reassigned to another place of service within the organization, or they may leave entirely. Therefore, when terminating the service of an unpaid staff member, follow the guidelines explained in previous chapters for terminating paid staff. If possible, reassigning them to a more suitable position of service is usually the best option.

Identifying the core reasons for why the unpaid staff member didn't succeed is critical. If the supervisor failed to provide appropriate support and resources, then forgiveness should be sought and granted. If the position was a mismatch—gifts and abilities didn't match the requirements of the position—then counsel the staff person into another position more suited for his or her abilities and personality. Affirm his or her strengths, talk about your knowing that he or she was sometimes frustrated with the current position, and then suggest that he or she might be more satisfied in another suggested position.

If something in their personal life contributed to the underperformance and it's appropriate for you to discuss this, mention that it might be best for them to get away from ministry for a period of time to concentrate fully on healing this personal need. If the problem is actually poor performance or an inability to embrace one's weaknesses, the supervisor needs to confront this lovingly, openly, and with a third party present. Analyze whether you can wait until the end of the one-year service agreement to allow this person to leave quietly. Waiting out the year isn't a bad choice, but don't simply default to this position—*choose it wisely*. If immediate action is required, the health of the ministry is too important to allow an underperforming staff person to damage the health of the institution. Remember to diligently follow the principles on dismissing staff explained previously in this book.

3. Unpaid staff members have more limitations on the time they can offer.

Carefully match the time required to successfully fulfill the duties of the position to the time the unpaid staff member can offer. It's incredibly frustrating and unfair to be told that a position requires five hours a week—and then discover that it actually takes ten. While this principle is also true for paid staff members, it's much more important when recruiting unpaid staff. You don't want them to think that you intentionally misled them when they were recruited. During the review process, discuss with unpaid staff members how much time they're investing on a weekly basis and whether this matches what they were previously told. If they are investing more hours, ask whether that is okay or they need your assistance in recruiting others to help. You also may need to assist them in reorganizing the position to more closely align with the communicated time commitment.

4. Unpaid staff members may expect a community or ministry team environment rather than a corporate-type setting.

Paid staff members desire to serve on a team where they're valued and can connect with fellow paid staff members. However, they don't desire the same level of community connection that unpaid staff members may expect. Many—if not most—unpaid staff members serve because they want to feel like they belong to a loving community and worthwhile team that's accomplishing important things for God's kingdom. Supervisors of unpaid staff teams need to recognize this value and create an environment of caring community with these unpaid staff members so that they feel cared for and connected to each other and the supervisor.

As personal needs arise among the unpaid staff, the supervisor needs to either provide pastoral care or recruit an unpaid staff member to serve on that team—someone who has the gifts of compassion and service and wants to express these gifts as a lay pastor to the team. When unpaid staff members suffer from personal crises and know that their fellow team members will rally around to provide loving and consistent support, they will serve their hearts out. You can't put a price on the salary these saints deserve.

A Final Word

Understanding the similarities and differences in building and supervising paid versus unpaid staff members is critical to the successful fulfillment of your organization's mission and vision. Supervisors who learn how to effectively lead unpaid staff teams will attract a large supply of talented and gifted people. Recruiting and mobilizing unpaid staff isn't technically part of our job; it is, however, our job as Christian leaders in most organizations and most definitely in all churches. Too many times we allow incorrect, prejudiced assumptions to hinder our ability to complete this task well.

I pray that you'll join me in prayerfully reflecting on how we might more effectively help those within the sphere of our organizations find engaging places of ministry—positions that will expand their ministry capacities and release the Spirit's passion in their hearts, minds, and souls. Furthering God's purposes within his kingdom depends on our getting this right! I would rather lead a small number of dedicated, passionate, unpaid staff members to tackle a huge challenge in God's kingdom than lead a large number of volunteers who are underperforming and serving out of guilt or other poor motives just so we can "keep the peace." Our churches and organizations deserve our best. And our unpaid staff members deserve that we ask the best of them.

Conclusion

How to Treat a Staff Infection

I discovered long ago that there's truly no "conclusion" to leading staff members. Staff teams are evolving organisms who follow a life and course of their own—even with the best of leadership. Effective leadership requires that we stay in the humble mode of a *learner*, regularly adjusting the ways we lead to fit the people in our organization.

One valuable lesson I've learned is the need to lead others in the manner that best serves the team, rather than the one that I might prefer. For example, I would generally choose to deliver information directly, straight up, and all at once. My experience has taught me, however, that many don't like receiving information that way. They may prefer that it be presented in a softer, more indirect manner, one that uses a more "manageable parcels" approach.

Another lesson in personal preference differences involves how one feels appreciated. I need few accolades or times of recognition. Instead, I desire to be trusted and respected in a way that allows me to do my job. If I can successfully move along the organization I'm leading, then I feel the most trusted and respected—and therefore the most appreciated. However, most staff members need more frequent acknowledgement and affirmation, so I need to adjust my leadership style accordingly. I also get bored easily and like a demanding and regularly changing environment, but that is the exact opposite of what many desire or find tolerable!

In light of these and other differences between a leader and his or her team, how do we best serve the organization and team members in a way that doesn't make it all about ourselves as the leaders? This must be our overriding strategy: everything needs to focus on *God's desires* for the organization. Therefore, we need to constantly ask ourselves, "What's the best way to mobilize our staff team to accomplish God's purposes?"

I'm not suggesting a "whack-a-mole" approach to leading staff, however! Remember that game at the arcades? You're given a rubber or foam mallet, and you whack as many moles as you can as they pop up randomly and quickly. Too many leaders operate this way, putting all their focus on the latest problems that pop up rather than the foundational principles that should guide their leadership. (The game just might be a great form of therapy for a frustrated staff, though!)

Another reason I'm finding it hard to conclude this discussion is the fact that God created us all to be unique, wonderful, and complex. Build a team of people and you exponentially increase that uniqueness, wonder, and complexity. I don't view myself as an expert on leading or serving with staff, but I do have more experience than most people. In my over thirty years of experience serving on and leading staff teams, I've developed many key principles which I've discussed in this book.

However, while many of these trusted principles are foundational for leading most staff challenges, I regularly find myself facing a totally new challenge—one that requires me to step back and approach it in a fresh and new way. My point? The uniqueness and complexity of teams mean that you can't use formulaic approaches or depend solely on your past experiences. Leading is always a combination of key principles from the past and new applications for the ever-changing new challenges of the future.

Therefore, give up the search for perfect responses or strategies to all or specific staff problems. They simply don't exist! Instead, stay focused on what you can and can't control. No one can regulate another person's response when being confronted. Yes, we can make it better or worse with our strategies and approach, but we can't control people or keep someone from being hurt when confronted. What we can influence is the godly, loving, and wise manner in which we do so.

Be proactive and principle driven. Identify what principles you judge are foundational when leading staff, and then follow these faithfully. At the same time, you must apply them wisely, because they don't fit every situation. One size doesn't fit all. Even your foundational principles need to be tailored to fit the actual situation you face.

May God bless you in your role as a staff member. I pray you'll find joy and satisfaction in faithfully and effectively serving on a staff team. May you always lead with godliness, humility, wisdom, courage, grace, mercy, respect, and love. As under-shepherds who report to the Head Shepherd—Christ himself—how else will we mobilize others to serve in God's kingdom with distinction? What an awesome responsibility!

Dr. Craig Williford is president of Denver Seminary. He has taught in college and seminary settings, and in his twenty-five years of pastoral experience he served in five churches. He is the author or coauthor of several books, including *Spiritual Formation in the Home*.

Carolyn Williford has written and coauthored seven books, including *Devotions for Families That Can't Sit Still*. She is also a teacher and speaker who is passionate about spiritual growth, reading, and hiking the mountains of Colorado.